PRAISE FOR *WEB-EMPOWER YOUR CHURCH*

Stephenson has truly unleashed the power of internet ministry for your church. If you're looking for a readable and educating book on web-empowered ministry, look no further. This book is it. I can't believe how much I learned from my first reading. I will be returning to the book over and over.
—Bill Easum, Author, Consultant, and President of Easum, Bandy & Associates

Mark Stephenson's *Web-Empower Your Church* is a comprehensive roadmap to starting and maintaining a successful team-based internet ministry at your church. Mark gives equal time to the human and technical sides of internet ministry. Buy and read this book to avoid the many pitfalls to starting an internet ministry.
—David Gillaspey, President of Great Church Websites

This book heralds a message that the church needs to hear: We must speak today's language, and that vernacular is online communication. Much like Gutenberg revitalized the gospel with a printing press, we can via the internet. Mark Stephenson has succinctly outlined this outreach strategy in *Web-Empower Your Church*.
—Nathan Smith, GodBit.com

Mark not only guides you through the process of building an internet ministry, but also builds your passion for its necessity and potential. Both the internet and God know no borders, and I'm blessed to serve as developer of software used by this international God-ordained mission to help web-empower churches.
—Kasper Skårhøj, Denmark, Creator of TYPO3

Stephenson has managed to do what so many other computer-savvy, online guru, geek-types have tried and failed to accomplish: write a book that opens the world of the internet to the church. *Web-Empower Your Church* is not just simple to read, it stands out as one of the premier introductions to how the church can effectively and near-easily expand its reach beyond its walls and exponentially into the world. Stephenson defines, explains, and illustrates the world wide web concisely enough for the novice, and yet the depth of his content provides an excellent primer on how to launch a church's foray into cyber ministry. Those who read *Web-Empower Your Church* and heed Stephenson's guidance have a unique opportunity to start something that may well have a global impact for the cause of Jesus Christ.
—Dr. Bill Tenny-Brittian, House Church Association and author

What can happen when a church really understands and harnesses the power of the internet? "CyberGuy" Stephenson leads us through the wealth of insight he has gained in ten years of developing his church's online ministry. If this does not whet your appetite, nothing will!
—Tony Whittaker, United Kingdom, InternetEvangelismDay.com

Web-Empower Your Church

UNLEASHING THE POWER OF INTERNET MINISTRY

Mark M. Stephenson
"Church CyberGuy"

Abingdon Press
Nashville

WEB-EMPOWER YOUR CHURCH:
UNLEASHING THE POWER OF INTERNET MINISTRY

Copyright © 2006 Mark Stephenson

All rights reserved.

This book is printed on acid-free paper.

Library of Congress Cataloging-in-Publication Data

Stephenson, Mark Morgan, 1960–
  Web-empower your church : unleashing the power of internet ministry / Mark M. Stephenson.
      p.   cm.
    ISBN 0-687-64284-1 (alk. paper)
  1. Internet—Religious aspects—Christianity.   2. Internet in church work.   I. Title.

BR99.74.S74   2006
253.0285'4678—dc22

                                                          2006031998

Scripture quotations, unless otherwise indicated, are from the *New Revised Standard Version of the Bible,* copyright © 1989, by the Division of Christian Education of the National Council of the Churches of Christ in the United States of America. Used by permission. All rights reserved.

06 07 08 09 10 11 12 13 14 15—10 09 08 07 06 05 04 03 02 01

MANUFACTURED IN THE UNITED STATES OF AMERICA

*To the innovators and
risk takers around the world
who maximize the gifts
God has given them
to take us all to new levels*

CONTENTS

GRATITUDES

I am indebted to many people who helped make this book and my life in ministry possible:

I thank my parents: Ralph and Caryl Stephenson for always believing I could do absolutely anything.

I thank my family: My wife Ellen, son Thomas, son Andrew, son Michael, and daughter Mya for allowing me to pursue this incredible adventure in ministry. And Ellen for the cover photo, and Andrew for his praying hands in the photo.

I thank Ginghamsburg Church: Pastor Mike Slaughter, staff, and lay leaders for creating an environment where ordinary followers of Jesus expect to do the extraordinary by the power of the Holy Spirit.

I thank the Ginghamsburg staff CyberGuys: Chris Boerger, Christian Crawford, and Jeremy Nash for dealing with the challenges I often cause and for working tirelessly for the Kingdom.

I thank the Ginghamsburg unpaid servants: Deanna Bishop, Jim Denney, Stan Gheen, Pat Hedleston, Kate Johnsen, Dawn Swinford, Jerry Warner, and many more for devoting your time and talents to serving and making our church internet ministry what it is today.

I thank the Foundation for Evangelism: Paul Ervin, Rubin Perry, Jack Ewing, Jane Wood, Lynda Leonard, and the Board for your wisdom, total devotion to offering Christ to the world, and the resources to make the Web-Empowered-Church God-dream a reality.

I thank the current and future Web-Empowered Church Team: Barbara Bowser, Jeff Segars, Dave Slayback, Brian Slezak, Glenn Kelley, and others for your technical expertise and willingness to serve churches around the world.

I thank the TYPO3 developer: Kasper Skårhøj from Denmark for listening to and following God and then devoting much of your life to creating the core software needed to web-empower the church.

FOREWORD

An "All Thumbs" Church

When I was a kid, to say that someone was "all thumbs" was not a compliment. It meant you were clumsy, klutzy, and just couldn't get it right.

What a difference a generation makes. Today kids celebrate those who are "all thumbs" for their ability to navigate the digital media world of iPods, controllers, TiVos, remotes, PDAs, cell phones, and the web.

If any book can get an "all thumbs" church to become "all thumbs," Mark Stephenson's *Web-Empower Your Church* is the one. For the last five hundred years, the primary delivery system for learning and faith development has been print. With Johannes Gutenberg's invention of moveable type, the printed Bible superseded the cathedral as the defining medium of Christianity. With Tim Berners-Lee's invention of the world wide web in 1989, the internet (which no one person invented) is becoming the defining medium of Christianity and the major delivery system for learning and faith development.

Unfortunately, the church's brain is so stuck on the print autopilot that it is almost the last one to recognize that the menu has changed. Just like codices opened up horizons for the church in the second century, and the printing press opened up new vistas in the sixteenth century, Stephenson shows how the web opens up a whole new missional world for the church in the twenty-first century, especially with our twenty-second century kids.

A young theological student came up to me after a lecture at his seminary. He warned me that I was a little behind the curve. I quickly agreed but found his chiding surprising since he bobbed his head approvingly when I encouraged those pastors and parents present to acquaint themselves with networking websites like MySpace and Facebook, where their kids are pioneering new ways of making connections and "friending" (which are not necessarily the same things as "friendships"). The "Top 8" default on a MySpace page would be a good place to begin, I suggested, since kids tend to judge each other by their "friends" list. The "Top 8" can be a huge source of anxiety and despair to teenagers, especially when Top 8 status isn't reciprocated.

Where I was behind, he said, was that the "Top 8" could now be reset for a "Top 4" or a "Top 12" or "Top whatever" I wanted to make it. What's more, he said, not all kids were using it as measure of social success or failure. In fact, the kids he worked with as their youth minister were starting to use the "Top 8" as a means of evangelism. Either they made their "Top 8" their personal prayer list, and listed those kids they were praying for the most, or they turned the "Top 8" on its head and filled it with the bottom 8. Those forgotten, ignored kids and "rejects" that didn't make any one else's list, the Christian kids put on their "Top 8."

But then he revealed something that reminded me how autopilot can sometimes be another word for crash-and-burn. The church where he served as youth minister refused to count the time he was online with his youth group as part of his twenty-hour-a-week position as "Youth Minister." That was personal time, not paid time. If he were to type personal letters to communicate with his kids, or to dictate such letters to the church secretary, that would be counted in his twenty-hour-a-week job description. But not online time.

The pain in his voice and eyes was palpable: "I'm not sure I can keep working for a church that is so far out of it," he said. "I love these kids. It's not a matter of hours. I'm glad to put in way more than twenty hours anyway. It's a matter of having your church understand its own kids, know what needs to be done to reach kids today, and celebrate the impact the gospel is having on these kids."

My hope and dream is that Mark Stephenson's book may help get the church off autopilot so it can fly into the future without losing its most missional and incarnational leaders. The church has been waiting for a book that "unleashes" the missional power of internet ministry for a long time. And this book was worth waiting for. With a humble spirit, humorous style and energizing confidence, Stephenson offers practical, field-tested templates for propelling the gospel into the twenty-first century on the www mission field.

It's a book that belongs in every pastor's library, but not on the shelf.

In the past, books were so valuable (especially theological texts) that they were sometimes bound in covers set with precious stones. This book is so valuable it deserves not a place on your shelf, but a place near your favorite chair. Instead of letters on the page written in gold, it needs to be underlined in ink and highlighted in multiple colors. What about those gem-studded covers? The covers of this book need the coffee stains and food marks and all thumb prints of study, attention, and affection.

Leonard Sweet
E. Stanley Jones Professor of Evangelism, Drew Theological School
Distinguished Visiting Professor, George Fox University
www.wikiletics.com

INTRODUCTION

Harness the power of the internet for Jesus. The internet is opening up new possibilities for all aspects of church ministry, from daily administrative tasks to worldwide evangelism and discipleship.

This book is about web-empowering your church ministries. Learn the practical steps, techniques, and ideas needed to develop an excellent and effective web ministry that increases your efficiency and effectiveness—your God-difference.

Mark Stephenson, Director of CyberMinistry and Technology at Ginghamsburg Church, shares his experiences with starting and now leading a large and active church web ministry. Ginghamsburg's website is now over four thousand pages in size, and averages over one new visit every half-minute, 24/7.

Whether your church has a website or not, this book will help you grow your internet ministry and take the next step to fully web-empower your church ministries. Visit www.WebEmpowered Church.com, where you can get the free software tools and support to make it happen.

The book includes a CD-ROM (for PC Windows) that will help you learn about, install, and evaluate the Web-Empowered Church software and the TYPO3 Content Management System. This software is all free and open source. Please visit the book webpages at www.WebEmpoweredChurch.com/book for a full list of website links mentioned in the book, additional information, updates, and a discussion forum. Post your questions to the discussion forum, where the author and Web-Empowered Church community will answer.

CHAPTER 1

MY CHURCH SAW NO NEED FOR THE INTERNET

How we struggled to start an internet ministry that the *Wall Street Journal* eventually featured

Wow! I am excited! A church website opens up so many possibilities for our church. And, as a person who loves to play with computers, I can't imagine anything more fun than doing computer stuff for the Kingdom. It is a match made in heaven. This is going to be awesome!

With these thoughts in mind, I skipped into the office of the Director of Communications at our church to tell him this exciting news. He told me that although it sounded interesting, someone else had already been working on it; and he suggested that I might be able help after that person got it started. I needed to wait, which was not fun, but at least I knew I would still get to work on the website. So I waited for a few months and exchanged e-mails now and then to monitor the apparent lack of progress. I also took that time to learn more about building church websites because I really had no clue how to do it. I had never even created a webpage. After multiple e-mails and a couple more visits, it was clear to me that a church website was far from a priority at our church. After all, our church had been around for over one hundred years without a website. Although they did not come out and say it, the attitude was "Why do we need one now?" To me, the future ministry possibilities for web ministry seemed endless. To them, at best, a website was a nice little novelty that might attract a few computer geeks to our church.

I prayed often and continued reading and learning. Then I did something that might not serve as wise advice for you. I decided to build our church website myself, without any help from the church. I found a church brochure and typed it into my computer. I scanned the church logo from the brochure and spent hours trying to doctor it up so it didn't look like I scanned it from the brochure. For that time and my skill level, the website looked okay, though I'd be embarrassed to show it to you now. I then met again with the Director of Communications. I told him I had created the initial website on my own and was about to register Ginghamsburg.org and post the website. I needed to know if the church was with me. The good news is that he chose to be with me and, in fact, helped me build a team to start the CyberMinistry. Neither of us knew the extent of the impact our website would have. A few years later media outlets including the *Wall Street Journal,* the *Dallas Morning Sun*, and *Fox News TV* would feature our church website.

Most people in church leadership positions know very little about internet ministry. Perhaps you feel the same as I did. You may be a pastor, a church staff member, or (like I was) an attendee attempting to serve. You see the need and potential for a church website, yet the church sees it as an unnecessary novelty. From my experience, I have learned that most people in church leadership positions know very little about internet ministry, or CyberMinistry, as we call it. As one pastor told me, "They don't teach this stuff in seminary." So first, it is important to help educate the church on this exciting ministry opportunity. Second, it is vital to be prayerfully and respectfully persistent. Unlike many other church ministries, internet ministry is not easily accepted by everyone in the congregation. Most other ministries in the church have been around for hundreds of years. Internet ministry is new and unknown. But we need to do what is right, even when we are not understood or fully supported. Please don't let naysayers stop you. The opportunity is too important. And it is really fun, too!

Internet Ministry Power

The internet is a powerful communications tool that you can use to dramatically increase the impact of your ministries. As you will learn throughout this book, most of the ministries in your church can be web-empowered in some way to improve effectiveness and efficiency. With the internet, you can:

1. improve church communication quickly, easily, and inexpensively;
2. empower lay volunteers for active participation;
3. minister to people at any time and in any place;
4. allow your sermons, devotions, and Bible studies to continue to minister for years to come;
5. expand your ministry to reach people around the world.

It is time for the church to fully harness the power of the internet for the kingdom of God. The result is likely to exceed your expectations. For example, we decided to put our sermons online. We began by recording, transcribing, editing, and then posting the sermon text and presentation graphics on our church website. A few months later, we were reviewing the website statistics provided by our hosting company. Among other things, website statistics can show the location of the internet service providers for the people who browse a website. As we examined the statistics, we were surprised to see that people were viewing our sermons from most of the fifty United States and from approximately twenty-five other countries. Wow, what a God-moment! This surprise gave us our first glimpse of what might be possible through CyberMinistry. Now, we commonly get visitors from over fifty different countries each month, and thousands of people view our sermons each week. In fact, we estimate that more people view our sermons online than the four thousand who see them at our church each week. The web has allowed a church located in a rural hundred-acre cornfield in Tipp City, Ohio, to minister to thousands of people all around the world! The same ministry power of the internet is available to your church as well.

> *It is time for the church to fully harness the power of the internet for the kingdom of God.*

About the Ginghamsburg Website

This book is based on our practical experiences with the initiation and development of the main Ginghamsburg Church website (www.Ginghamsburg.org) and a few smaller websites created for our other ministries. Our main website went online in January 1997. Since that time, the website has grown an average of one page per day, now totaling over four thousand pages. Most of the size is due to the online sermons, devotions, and Bible studies. The website also includes multiple years of weekly sermons in streaming video format. In 2006, the entire website occupies over forty gigabytes of disk space and receives over seventy thousand visits each month. These statistics make Ginghamsburg.org one of the largest and most-visited "local church" websites in the world.

In this book, I'd like to share with you some of what we have learned on our journey to creating this exciting ministry. When we started, we weren't professional web developers. We were unpaid church attendees with busy lives and full-time, non-web-related day jobs. We didn't hire a company or consultant to help us. When our website went live, our church budget for Cyber-Ministry was about $25 per month. We learned on our own, making plenty of mistakes along the way. This book is for churches with limited resources and limited experience. That's where we came from, too.

This book is for churches with limited resources and limited experience.

Ten Excuses for Why Churches Don't Have Websites

Even as the internet has grown in popularity and importance in daily life, many churches remain hesitant to start or revitalize an internet ministry. Here are ten common reasons for not having a church website. Each excuse includes a brief response that may be helpful to you as you educate the people in your church about internet ministry.

1. Churches Don't Need Websites.

It is correct that our churches do not need websites to function. But our churches do need websites to be more effective and to reach more people, which we all should want to do. God has allowed us access to this powerful communication tool, so we should apply it appropriately to enhance our mission. Just as Jesus stood in a boat or on a hillside to increase the people's ability to see and hear him, we should apply available resources to help others see and hear God speak and minister through our churches.

As the internet becomes more commonplace, people expect churches to have websites. Today, not having at least a simple church website is like not listing your church in the phone book or not having a sign in front of your church building. We commonly hear from people whose first exposure to our church was through our website. More people everyday look to the internet as their primary source of information, and that includes looking for a church.

Today, not having at least a simple church website is like not listing your church in the phone book.

Here is one example: Due to a job transfer, a husband and wife were making plans to move to Ohio. Searching the web for information on communities and churches, they found our church website. Based on information presented on our website, they made the decision to move into our area just so they could attend our church. They began viewing our streaming-video sermons each week, and they read much more about our church on the website. By the time they arrived at the door of our church, many of the common barriers to assimilation in the church were gone. They would not be attending our church if they had not already "e-attended" our church.

2. The Internet Is Filled with Sin.

For many people, the issue is fear of the unknown and the dark side of the internet. Through newspapers and television we hear of an internet filled with pornography, hate groups, computer viruses, spam, and scams. Sin abounds on the public internet just as it does in other forms of public communication. The sin and evil found on the internet are all the more reason for every church to have a website. Jesus hung out with those who sinned and who did not believe. Each church should be where the needy people are found. We want our website to be right in the midst of the sin-filled websites that we hear about. For example, when a person goes to an internet search engine looking for meaning or answers or fun, we want our church webpage links to be intermingled with links to the sin-filled website pages because perhaps that person will click on our website link instead of others. We ought to be where the people in need are, and many of them are on the internet.

3. It's Just Not Our Thing.

Clearly, not every church is called to produce a four-thousand-page website with multiple gigabytes of streaming video. Some churches are called to transport hundreds of children to church in a bus ministry; others to set up a large shelter for the homeless; and others to help young, unwed mothers. Different churches are called to different missions based on their gifts and resources as well as the community they serve. However, due to the power of the internet and the expectations of the people you serve, your church should have at least a simple website that provides some basic information and functions like an electronic yellow pages ad.

4. We Can't Keep the Website Up-to-Date.

These words are far too common: "We created our church website a long time ago, but it is totally out of date and no one ever looks at it." If it is registered with search engines, people have probably looked at it; and they may have been turned off or misled. The only thing worse than not having a church website is having a website that is out of date. Incorrect websites are misleading, and they are a negative reflection on your church. A website is not a project to be done and then left alone. A website is an ongoing ministry that requires commitment—just like other forms of church communication that are updated as changes occur. If your church website is not up-to-date, then your church is missing a ministry opportunity.

The only thing worse than not having a church website is having a website that is out of date.

5. The Internet Is Only for the Rich.

More and more people have internet access at home, at work, or in public facilities such as libraries, but it is unlikely that everyone you serve has access, and some of those who do have access may have poorly equipped computers or slow internet connections. To help people without internet access, we added kiosks at the church so people can visit our website. Perhaps a ministry opportunity exists at your church to equip and train people to use computers and the internet.

Always make important information available in both electronic and non-electronic formats.

In any case, always make important information available in both electronic and non-electronic formats. This allows people without easy internet access or people who prefer paper versions to receive information. For example, we offer our church newsletter in both electronic format (via e-mail) and paper format. We ask that people volunteer to receive only the electronic copy; otherwise, they receive a paper copy.

6. It's Too Expensive to Maintain a Website.

Of all the ministries in the church, an internet ministry is usually one of the most cost effective. The internet gives our church access to the world. The potential of internet ministry is huge! To have a church website, you don't need expensive internet connections or the latest computers. You may be able to host your website for free or a reduced rate with a local internet hosting company, your denomination's hosting services, or a church website hosting company. Otherwise, you can usually purchase hosting from a web hosting company for less than $25 per month. And in most cases, the computers and internet access you have either at the church or at home are sufficient to create the website. Internet ministry is worth the modest cost, and it can sometimes save money by reducing printing and mailing costs.

> *Of all the ministries in the church, an internet ministry is usually one of the most cost effective.*

7. We Don't Have Anyone with the Skills.

People with computer skills and interests traditionally have had few opportunities to use their gifts and passions in the church. Most churches have at least one person with the technical skills and/or interest to develop a church website. This offers them a great opportunity for service. In addition, the technical barriers are coming down as more powerful tools and instructional resources become available. With this book, for example, we hope to share what we have learned through our experiences to help you develop the skills you need to build an active and productive internet ministry.

8. Online Ministry Keeps People away from Church.

Internet ministry, television ministry, and radio ministry have been criticized for encouraging people not to participate in a church where they can worship, have fellowship, and serve together in community. God designed us as social creatures with a need for other people, and a full Christian life includes relationships with

A church internet ministry should teach and encourage physical participation in the church.

fellow believers. We have talked with many of our website visitors, and they tell us that the website augments their Christian growth and does not replace church attendance. In any case, a church internet ministry should teach and encourage physical participation in the church. An internet ministry does not and will not replace the physical importance of a church community. The internet cannot think, love, or physically hug. In fact, a successful internet ministry enables a church to be more effective and results in even more opportunities to interact in a personal way.

9. Technology Is Cold and Impersonal.

When telephone answering machines first became available, many people disliked them and would not leave messages. They would say, "I'm not going to talk to a dumb machine." Now, the response to these devices is quite different. We receive long, detailed messages that sometimes don't even require us to call back. The fundamental capabilities provided by answering machines (or voicemail) are the same. So what changed? People adapted to this new form of communication. God designed us to be incredibly adaptive creatures, capable of maximizing the effectiveness of any communication technology. New communication technologies often feel cold and impersonal until we adapt to them. E-mail and instant messaging seem quite strange and even unusable to new users until they adapt. But for many people, once they become familiar with the technology, the messages almost shoot off their fingers into cyberspace. Before e-mail, you could never have convinced me that I would prefer to type rather than to talk on the phone; however, I now often choose e-mail instead of the telephone. Communication technology that connects people does not stay cold or impersonal for long.

10. It Is Too Time-Consuming.

Like most things that make a difference, internet ministry takes a great deal of time and effort, but I hope this book will help significantly by allowing you to focus on creating and growing the ministry instead of spending time figuring out what to do. This ministry can be done from anywhere there is a computer with internet access, and it can also be done at any time. It is a ministry that is well suited for busy people and people who are free to work only at odd hours. In fact, I still work from home even though I lead the ministry. As a team, we use our home computers, work on the website when we can fit in the time, communicate most details via e-mail, and meet in person occasionally just to talk.

The Web-Empowered Church Can Help!

The good news is that you are not alone in this internet ministry adventure. I direct a ministry called the Web-Empowered Church (WEC) that is here to help you. (See WebEmpowered Church.com for more information.) WEC is a ministry of the Foundation for Evangelism (Evangelize.org). The mission of WEC is to innovatively apply WEB technology to EMPOWER the worldwide CHURCH for ministry. The book you are reading, WEC online teaching, and WEC community forums all provide support to churches that are building websites. The community forums bring together internet-ministry servants from churches around the world. Most importantly, WEC provides powerful, open source web software that you can use for your church or Christian ministry website. And the WEC software costs you nothing. Yes, it is free! The WEC software runs on a web server on the public internet, and it allows you to create and maintain your church website with powerful ministry features. The software has special webpages that allow you to create your website from a standard web browser on your PC. No special software is required. With a proper username and password, you can make updates to your website from any computer connected to the internet. In fact, multiple people from your church can help maintain your website.

The WEC software costs you nothing. Yes, it is free!

The WEC software uses a free Content Management System (CMS) called TYPO3. TYPO3 does all the work of storing the content, appearance, and functionality of your webpages. Based on information you enter, the CMS automatically generates the webpages for people visiting your church website.

Churches around the world are already using the WEC software. You do not need to use WEC to benefit from this book, but I will share more about the features of TYPO3 and WEC throughout the following chapters.

Doing the God Thing

Perhaps my journey into internet ministry will help you see how God is working in your journey. I am an electrical engineer by training and have worked for several years in computer-related research, largely for the United States Air Force. When I came to Ginghamsburg Church, they did not have a website; and as I mentioned before, they did not really know why they would want one. Since my wife and I were new to the church, we attended membership classes where we took a test to help identify our gifts. The goal was to help us connect with a servant opportunity that fit our God-given gifts. They told us that if we connected to the right ministry, then we would naturally enjoy it and draw energy from it. In short, we'd love it! The problem was that the available opportunities did not fit me. After additional thought and prayer, I felt that I needed to start an internet ministry. Now that would energize me! Internet ministry has at times been very tough; the hours have been long, and it has been frustrating. However, since this ministry is my passion, I continue to love it, to draw energy from it, and to be blessed to serve here. I encourage you to "do the God thing." I don't mean do a good thing for God, but instead get involved with a ministry about which you are passionate and for which God has gifted you.

Get involved with a ministry about which you are passionate and for which God has gifted you.

Doing the God thing can be intimidating at times, but it is a real blessing to serve and be used by God for a divine purpose. As I continued to work to grow the ministry, our pastor, Michael Slaughter told us he felt God telling him that our church would minister to ten thousand people by the year 2000. We realized that God was going to meet this goal in a non-traditional way because we did not have either the space at the church or the local population to achieve this goal through traditional church attendance. Instead, God could allow us to minister to many thousands of people through our website. It is impossible to know exactly how many different people our website has ministered to, but all indications are that we met this ambitious goal in the year 2000.

If internet ministry is your God thing, then I encourage you to just do it! You may or may not have the full support of church leadership. For me, the support from church leadership started modestly but grew stronger as we all learned more about the ministry potential of the internet. From my discussions with other would-be internet ministry leaders, it appears that few church leaders are ready to jump into internet ministry. Many have limited understanding of this type of ministry, and many are what my friend calls "TechNo"—they know little about technology, which is intimidating to them. Starting an internet ministry often begins with an education process. It's a little bit scary and a little bit different, but we need to go forward because the potential ministry impact is huge!

An internet ministry can also be good stewardship of your church's gifts, time, and resources. For example, pastors often spend many hours prayerfully crafting sermons. These sermons are usually shared with only a portion of the congregation on a given weekend. By using the internet, you can make the sermon available to others both in and out of the congregation, now and in the future. People have sent us e-mails stating that content on our website has changed their lives. Many times, these people live hundreds of miles away, and the content they reference is months or even years old. Without the internet, they probably never would have experienced this benefit. And we are blessed to be able to share the gifts God has given us. It is a blessing to do the God thing.

An internet ministry can also be good stewardship of your church's gifts, time, and resources.

CHAPTER 2

I ALMOST KILLED OUR NEWBORN CYBERMINISTRY

The hard lessons I learned about building an effective CyberTeam

*Okay, let's get started! We've got the go-ahead to get our internet
ministry going, but it seems like we need more people.
There are so many things to do: the technical stuff to figure out,
the graphic design (not my gift for sure), the navigation/
organization, the photos, and the content writing. This requires
diverse skills and knowledge. I don't have all of the skills and
knowledge, nor do I have the time to do all of this.*

We got some cookies and punch, put an ad in the church bulletin, and invited people to come after church to a meeting where they could learn about and join our new internet ministry. I waited in the room praying that God would send someone. People began to arrive. Then more people arrived. Then even more people arrived. We quickly opened the room divider to expand the room, and we hurried to get more chairs. The cookies and punch were gone in microseconds. The stress of it all probably blotted out my memory, but I think there were about fifty people there. It felt like thousands! Once the mob was seated, we talked about what we wanted to do with our newborn CyberMinistry. The turnout was much better than we had expected, and we were not sure what to do with all the people. We got a list of their names and e-mail addresses, thanked them for coming, and got out of there before the mob turned hostile.

The good news is that internet ministry intrigues people, many of whom will at least come to a meeting to check it out. The challenge is that you need to be ready for them when they come. We were not ready, but the one thing we had totally right was a desire to do internet ministry with a team.

The Secret to an Excellent Internet Ministry

I believe that the success we've seen with our church website has little to do with technology and everything to do with team-based ministry. Beginning or growing an effective internet ministry should start by building a team that can carry out the many diverse tasks that such a ministry entails. An effective and sustained internet ministry requires teamwork for two main reasons. First, growing and maintaining the website takes a lot of time—people must gather, create, organize, edit, and post the content. People must also research technical details and implement solutions. Second, internet ministry requires many different skills and gifts, and God does not stuff all these gifts into one person. God created us to be interdependent. One result of not having a complete and effective team is a web ministry that starts with a flurry of activity, generates some webpages (even great webpages), and then goes dormant. The result is a common church website phenomenon: the webpages have not been updated for months. The website says, "Come to our Christmas Program," but it is July. Without an effective team, the ministry can lose momentum as members tire because they are overworked or are working outside of their passion, gifts, and interests. Beginning with a strong team is the best way to get started and the best way to keep the ministry going for the long haul.

An effective and sustained internet ministry requires teamwork.

In addition to starting with a team, it is important to remember that this activity is an "internet ministry" and not "website development." The word "development" implies a project that can be completed. A church website is never complete, just like children's ministry and worship are never complete. The word "ministry" implies an ongoing activity within the church. We are never done with ministry. A website is a living, changing, and evolving thing. And it takes a team to keep it alive.

Adding a web development company or paid staff to your team could accelerate the process, but it is not required or even recommended. Most church budgets are not ready to support the added cost, especially in the early stages, and even very small churches can create an internet ministry team from within the congregation. If you prefer, only low-level staff involvement is needed. We built our team of unpaid volunteers, called CyberServants, and created our first one thousand webpages before any paid person created a single page for our website. After the ministry got too busy, I transitioned from unpaid CyberMinistry Team Leader to paid Director of CyberMinistry. I worked just one day per week for the church, and, as you might guess, I continued to log quite a bit of unpaid servant time, too.

When our website surpassed two thousand pages, we hired our first full-time web staff person, and at about three thousand pages we added a designer. However, a critical responsibility of the staff is keeping our lay people tasked and supported. Although paid staff build many of our webpages (especially time-critical pages), provide supervision and guidance, and often supply content, our approach remains lay-driven. CyberServants supply most of the people power that makes our ministry go. I encourage you to build your team with mostly unpaid CyberServants. It saves money, but, more importantly, it provides a unique opportunity for people to participate in a ministry that can reach the world. Serving together in a team as we serve others helps us all grow in Christ.

Serving together in a team as we serve others helps us all grow in Christ.

The Kinds of Gifts We Need

Getting the right skill/gift mix among members of the team is important. There is more to building an internet ministry than gathering up all the computer-savvy people in your church. In fact, you will probably find that the majority of your team does not need to be computer savvy. An effective team commonly comprises the following roles. In most cases, the team will start small, and team members will take on more than one role.

The majority of your team does not need to be computer savvy.

> **Leader:** A leader articulates vision, motivates the team, and establishes direction and priorities. The leader decides what is posted on the website. The leader does not need to be a computer wiz but does need to have an understanding and appreciation for the significance of internet ministry. Pastors or communications leaders may serve in this role.

Manager: A manager keeps track of the many details associated with carrying out this ministry. The manager assigns tasks, monitors progress, and keeps the team healthy and moving forward. The manager typically needs some technical skills to be able to support the technical tasks.

Content Manager: A content manager understands the website content, can prompt others for information, and is in tune with the many activities going on in the church. The content manager verifies the accuracy and quality of the website and gets update requests and content to the other members of the team. In many ways, this is the most challenging role on the team. The lead church administrator often fits well here.

Writer and Editor: Writers and editors create the textual content and support the organization of the website. They are often forgotten on web teams, but without them the website literally has nothing to say. Writers and editors can be part of other ministries but need to be able to commit time to the internet ministry team.

Designer: A designer or graphic artist creates the overall appearance and page layout of the website as well as the graphics and photos. They may also be photographers or animators. A website is very visual, and the appearance of your website is the first thing visitors see, so it is a blessing to have a gifted graphic designer on the team.

Media: A media worker creates, records, and edits audio and video for the website. This job includes digitizing the audio or video so it can be played from your website. Adding media to your website is optional but increasingly important as faster internet connections enable websites to deliver quality media without long download times and media becomes more common throughout the internet.

Content Entry: A content entry worker creates and edits content on the pages of your website. New tools, such as content management systems, have made this a task that requires only basic computer skills. Most people who can use a computer can be taught to do content entry. Content entry also requires a visual eye for the look of the page and proofreading skills to make sure the additions or changes are correct.

Web Developer: A web developer creates the more advanced webpages and converts and reformats content. For example, a web developer would resize, crop, or slice up graphics. A developer must understand HyperText Markup Language (HTML) and Cascading Style Sheets (CSS). (See chapter 6.) Sometimes a web developer will use a scripting language such as JavaScript. Web developers often work with designers to implement the appearance of the website.

Programmer: A programmer develops active webpages that can perform dynamic functions, such as looking up information stored in a database and displaying it on a webpage. Programmers can also write software to automate various tasks, such as reformatting data and automatically generating webpages. Most churches do not need programmers unless they plan to create new web applications.

Server Manager: A server or network manager, often known as the "webmaster," manages the website computer. Depending on your web hosting options, the server manager has different specific duties. In general, the server manager configures, monitors, and backs up the server computer. This includes management of all the data and files on the computer as well as the software that performs functions such as serving webpages and e-mail. Most churches do not need a server manager because these services are provided automatically by web hosting companies.

A newer team may not need media, programmer, or server manager roles, but the other roles are important from the start. Of course, the roles can be shared and mixed to match the skills, gifts, and time availability of team members. In a smaller team, these functions may be combined into roles for two or three people, but as the team grows, the functions will spread across more people. Setting aside my solo/rebellious/feeble/embarrassing initial attempt at internet ministry, three people with varied skills started our Cyber-Ministry. The makeup of the team can vary substantially, but in general, an internet ministry team needs to have people that fulfill the roles listed above.

One note of caution: I have discussed the issue with several churches that have chosen a young person to lead and create their website simply because that person understands internet technology. This has not always worked well. A young, tech-savvy person can be a great addition to the team but may not be the best choice for a leadership role. The church website is a window into your church, so it is important to

The church website is a window into your church, so it is important to ensure that the website properly represents your church.

31

ensure that the website properly represents your church. A team leader must be well-equipped to make those decisions.

The current Ginghamsburg CyberMinistry team provides an operational example. Of course, our team is large now, but looking at the makeup of the team may be helpful. The main CyberMinistry team has fifteen committed members. Ten of them actively participate and the other five are semi-active. Most of the main team does content entry or media, and a few do some web developer, programmer, and server manager functions. Due to its insatiable appetite for web content, the CyberMinistry team has spawned two additional content teams. The first is the sermon transcription team—about five people who start with an audio tape of our weekend sermon and systematically transcribe and edit the sermon into a form suitable for reading on the web. The second team is the reflections team—roughly twenty-five unpaid servants who produce daily, Bible-based reflections for the website.

Approximately twice as many people produce content targeted for our website than build webpages.

Approximately twice as many people produce content targeted for our website than build webpages. In addition, most of the people in the main CyberTeam are not web developers, programmers, or server managers. The technical part of internet ministry often attracts the most attention, but as discussed in the next chapter, the majority of the effort in an excellent internet ministry is focused on content.

Getting People on the Team

There are multiple ways to recruit new members for the team. There are no set rules, but we have tried several techniques. Some worked well; others did not.

First, as described earlier, we tried the "bulletin blast" approach that resulted in a mob of fifty excited people interested in becoming CyberServants. This did not work out well. We were not prepared for such a large group, and most of these people had no experience doing anything other than browsing the web. We learned that few were ready for the time commitment that internet ministry requires. We discovered that although many people were interested in the internet (and the cool sounding name, CyberMinistry), most were not equipped to support the team. The key lesson we learned was that, especially for the more technical tasks, a significant part of internet ministry includes training the servants.

A significant part of internet ministry includes training the servants.

The next technique we tried was designed both to recruit and to train. Since the interest among people in the church seemed high but the technical skill level seemed low, we decided to offer a web development class during the normal Sunday school time. Putting together the thirteen-week class took a lot of work, but the participation was high. Again, we had filled a room with excited people. The class was a valuable service and a truly enjoyable experience. But it did not yield a single addition to our CyberMinistry team! When the class was over, everyone thanked us profusely, but no one wanted to join the team. Since it takes a great deal of effort to put together a class that is not likely to result in more Cyber-Servants, we no longer use such classes as a recruiting technique.

We currently use two methods of recruiting. First, we have a ministry within our church that helps people identify their unique gifts and get connected to other ministries within the church. This connection team sends us the names and contact information for people who are potentially a good fit for participation in our Cyber-Ministry. We even automated this process by creating an online servant catalog that helps people find the right place to serve. Second, we use bulletin announcements when we have a significant need for someone with a specific skill. For example, an announcement might read: "Sermon transcriptionist needed to help transcribe sermon audio into text format to support our internet ministry" or "Person knowledgeable in server-side scripting (PHP and MySQL) needed for our growing CyberMinistry." These two approaches tend to yield a higher percentage of people with a real desire and capability to serve.

Matching people to tasks works best when the match is based on individual gifts and passion. Look for what excites folks about this ministry, and put them there even if it requires extra effort or if other needs seem more urgent. We ask people who love children's ministry to help maintain the children's section of the website. We

Matching people to tasks works best when the match is based on individual gifts and passion. ask a person who is very busy but gets up early each morning for devotion and prayer to monitor the daily devotional e-mail and resend it when it does not work. His help is invaluable to the team because he catches problems before most of us even wake up, but more importantly he has an opportunity to serve in a ministry he is passionate about, even with his busy work schedule. We match people—those who enjoy working with video, participating in the motorcycle ministry, taking photographs at youth events, proofreading and editing, scheduling tasks, entering sermons, and more—to needs within CyberMinistry. The collective benefit of us all working as a team, each operating within individual gifts and passions, is amazing.

Equipping and Training Team Members

We require everyone in the CyberMinistry to have a computer with internet access and to legally own the software we use. We do this to keep costs down and because it would be difficult to track and manage church-owned items as people transition in and out of this ministry. Most people who want to participate in an internet ministry already have a computer and internet access. Many already have the software as well. We occasionally purchase unique, special-purpose items for people who are already actively participating on the team. For example, we purchased expensive video digitizing/editing software and a large dedicated hard drive for the team member who digitizes our sermon video.

Because we ask people to provide their own software, we use free or less expensive tools. The content entry people use Microsoft Word to extract the text from Word documents and a simple graphics editor to resize and crop images. They enter the content for our website using a web browser. Our more highly skilled web developers use tools like Dreamweaver and PhotoShop. People use many different tools, so we try not to use unique features that would force use of a specific tool.

Once they are properly equipped, many team members must be trained. Mentoring is the most effective training method we have found. When a person joins the ministry, we identify a task that he or she can accomplish while working with a mentor: a team member who is more experienced at the task. The mentor usually starts with a brief meeting to show the new team member how to do the task on a computer. Over time, the mentor remains available via phone, e-mail, or instant message to review the work and to answer questions. We have successfully mentored people with minimal computer skills, helping them become productive members of the team. They can even teach others! The process is not easy, but it has worked for us. We will work with any person who has the capability to learn and is willing to put forth the effort to become a significant contributor to the ministry.

Mentoring is the most effective training method we have found.

In addition to mentoring, we have an online reference called the "CyberMinistry Intranet." It is called an "intranet" because it is used exclusively for our internal team. Our CyberMinistry Intranet contains key information for team members: information about meetings, points of contact, expectations, websites for learning, software tools, guidelines/standards that ensure consistency across the website, conventions for file naming and file location, and more. We expect everyone on the team who builds pages to follow these guidelines. Most presentation settings, including fonts, colors, and layout, are controlled automatically with style sheets and page templates, but the guidelines explain the range of available and acceptable options for creating webpages. Online tutorials are another part of the CyberMinistry Intranet. We use a free tool called Wink to generate a series of animated and annotated screen shots designed to teach users how to perform tasks such as entering the transcribed sermon text onto our website.

The CyberMinistry Intranet also includes detailed descriptions of the processes we use to get content on the web. Documenting processes helps people know how their activities fit into the larger scheme. For example, we document each step required to take the weekly sermon from recorded audio to online transcribed-and-edited text pages. In the description of the processes, we include bits of information that help a person quickly jump in and become a fully capable contributor. For example, we include the video encoding settings we use when we create video for the website.

This information has been a powerful tool for enabling new members of the team to become productive quickly.

When someone is being mentored, the intranet can be a teaching tool. The intranet can also eliminate the need to answer the same questions over and over as new people come to the ministry. We recommend that you create at least a few pages on your website where you can place this sort of information.

The Team Culture of *We*

It is important to maintain a team culture dedicated to excellence. We are a team, so we use the language of a team. We always say that *we* do things. We say, "*We* updated the…," even if only one person made the change. *We* added a new feature. *We* messed up. *We*, *We*, *We*. There are very few of us who enhance or

We are a team, so we use the language of a team.

modify the website without another team member contributing in some way. Even the leader behaves and performs in the context of a healthy supportive team.

Also, we are God's instruments, giving God the credit. For this reason, it is very important to establish a culture of excellence. While we are far from perfect, God deserves only our best. This is why we do not post pages that do not meet our standards. We work with authors to make the pages right. We ask others to review and test our pages. We ask everyone on the team to be on the lookout for errors. Because the creation of webpages entails so many details, it is extremely easy to make a mistake. And we have made some big mistakes over the years! For example, when our church changed worship celebration times, we forgot to update that information in all the places it appeared on the website. Someone drove over one

It is very important to establish a culture of excellence.

hundred miles to visit our church, and the worship service was over. Another time we replaced the front page of the website with a blank page, and did not notice for hours. We have made mistakes that have crashed the server many times.

Mistakes will happen. The key is to catch and fix errors as early as possible. As a rule, we immediately drop everything else to fix an error. And we work as a team: the errors and fixes are team errors and team fixes. *We* make the mistakes, and *we* fix them. This culture of excellence, and teamwork makes mistakes less personal and less frequent.

Go, Team, Go!

Every step we take together is preceded, conducted, and concluded in prayer. Our CyberMinistry is to be a God thing. We pray for specific needs within the team, and those prayers will typically be answered in God's time. When someone new comes to the team, we assume God has a purpose for him or her, although that purpose may not immediately be revealed. So we never rush to place a person. It is not about filling empty slots. We want the Lord to drive our ministries, and we merely go where God leads. When we are recruiting and incorporating people into the team, we are always looking for God's leading and God's timing. If we can't fill a slot, we continue to pray and ask God to send the right person or guide us to the right solution.

> *Every step we take together is preceded, conducted, and concluded in prayer.*

Meeting and praying together is also important. The frequency of our team meetings depends on the current projects and the influx of new team members, but we recommend meeting in person at least once per month. We use the in-person meetings for orienting new team members, conducting occasional technical discussions, and getting to know people better. We don't need many meetings. Instead, we communicate online using a private CyberMinistry Team forum. We also communicate one-on-one via standard e-mail, instant message, and Skype (free voice over IP). Using these technologies, we are able to communicate as needed, sometimes multiple times per day for specific projects.

We use our online community to share our vision and plans so everyone knows where we are going and why. We also enjoy sharing encouraging e-mails that we receive from those who visit our website. Internet ministry can feel lonely now and then, and sometimes you wonder if anyone is out there in cyberspace. Personal e-mails are a great boost to the team, reminding us that this is about ministry, not HTML and other technical stuff. We are ministering to real people who need Jesus and who need to grow in Christ. Their e-mails help us know that our efforts are reaping Kingdom benefits.

A monthly report summarizing the ministry activities is also beneficial. Each month we produce a report that is e-mailed to our senior staff leadership and to the CyberMinistry Team and posted on the forum. The monthly report is an excellent tool for educating the church leadership on the significance of our ministry. Most senior staff members do not have background and training in internet ministry, so this report helps them understand our ministry impact. In the report, we list the team members and summarize various features and statistics for each portion of our website. For example, we list the number of website visitors, online subscribers, e-cards sent, prayer requests posted, and cell-group sign-ups. We include statistics from previous months so we can compare to the current month. Perhaps most importantly, we include copies of e-mails we have received from website visitors. These personal

Personal e-mails help our leadership and our team understand this ministry's impact on real people. e-mails help our leadership and our team understand this ministry's impact on real people. We are also a teaching church, so we commonly exchange e-mail with leaders of other church internet ministries, and these e-mails show the impact of our teaching ministry. (In order to protect the privacy of those who send us e-mail, we remove identifying information from the e-mail text.)

Of course, the real activity of internet ministry is not the meetings or the reports; it is the frequent additions and changes to the website. Most churches will update their website at least once a week, and many (including us) make changes nearly every day. Keeping this process going can be a challenge. We need to make sure information is flowing to the team at the appropriate times. We need to send web content to the appropriate team member who can prepare it and post it to the website. We need to help team members if they have questions. We need to review changes added by team members. We need to work with team members if there are issues with their work. And, we need to post the changes. The only team members who are allowed to post to the website directly are those who are experienced and have demonstrated excellence.

As we communicate with the team, we also work to support each team member emotionally and spiritually. Webpages can wait if we need to support a team member. Keeping our team healthy and strong is vital to the ongoing ministry, so we commonly exchange e-mails that have nothing to do with websites. We exchange prayer requests and general chatter about ordinary happenings. I keep a prayer list for team members and often pray for the team as a whole, individual team members, their families, and the ministry. Because the team can function as a small cell group, we also visit team members and their loved ones in hospitals, or at funerals. As you make more of a difference in a ministry, it often seems as though the enemy, or sin, seems to attack more. So it is vital to keep both yourself and the team emotionally and spiritually strong.

Webpages can wait if we need to support a team member.

CHAPTER 3

They Don't Care about Fancy Graphics and Technology

It's not the HTML code, but what is between the HTML tags, that matters.

It's time to build our website. I'm a high-technology kind of guy, and God really deserves something spectacular. I am determined to create the coolest, most high-tech church website in the world. We will have every technology trick in the book and a few more that we invent ourselves. We will include JavaScript, moving pictures, random pictures, mouseovers, dropdowns, pop-ups, scrolling text, XHTML, XML, RSS, SQL, PHP, CSS and every other letter combination out there. The graphics are going to be spectacular. The buttons will look like shimmering gold, and the website will look like it is in three dimensions including blending, shadows, shining, and reflections. When people see it, they will stand in awe.

I set out to build an award-winning church website with all the bells and whistles you can imagine. The initial version was a rather painful adventure that took ten times longer than expected, but I created something that started us down the path. It looked pretty cool on my computer. I uploaded it to my website and headed for the church to show it off and to receive praise and awe from the staff. The painful lessons began as awe turned to awful. First, the front page took forever to download over a modem. Then, the pages would not fit on small monitors. On the 256-color monitors at the church, all the cool shading was converted to a huge mosaic of polygons, and the textured background looked horrible. And, the JavaScript that did the scrolling text did not work with the browser they used.

Over the years I have learned more about the use of graphics and technology. The bottom line is that great websites are not great because of spectacular designs or the latest technologies (even though those shimmering gold buttons looked pretty cool). People care most about what is between the HTML tags—the content! Appearance and technology are there to enhance the presentation of the content, but content is the key.

It's All about Content

Think about the websites you visit frequently. Why do you go? People don't return to a website over and over because of the graphic design and the technology. Google is among the most-visited websites in the world, and it does not look fancy—it is rather boring. The draw to Google is that the user can rapidly and easily get a list of web links. We are drawn to Google because of the content it provides for us. The websites we visit over and over are those that provide content we care about. As we start to build an outstanding church website, our main focus should be on content. At Ginghamsburg Church, the most popular sections of our website are sermons, Bible studies, and devotionals. The majority of content that people really want is in these sections. Content can also come from an interactive feature such as an online forum. But having the coolest forum technology will not draw people unless there is exchange of content; even the interactive features are all about the content inside them.

> *The websites we visit over and over are those that provide content we care about.*

Who Is Your Church Website Audience?

Content is key, but the content must be relevant to the visitor. A website may be filled with information, but if people don't care about the information, then they don't care about the website. The first step in deciding what content to add is deciding who forms your audience. Leaders in your church who understand your mission and vision for ministry can best make this decision. They may do so by answering questions like: Whom do we want coming to our website? Whom are we speaking to? Whom do we want to serve? Your website might serve some of the following groups: potential attendees, attendees, members, church leaders, pre-Christians, Christians, anti-Christians, children, youth, college students, senior adults, single parents, singles, married, divorced, depressed, lonely, blind, deaf, and bikers. You might say, "We want to serve them all." That would probably be impossible to do effectively with a single website (or congregation). Most churches would find it difficult to generate the content needed to serve all these groups.

Who do we want coming to our website? Who are we speaking to? Who do we want to serve?

Let's say you want to create a website to help children grow in Christ. Clearly this website will be different from one designed to reach isolated and lonely adults. The appearance, content, organization, and features will all be dramatically different for each of these target audiences. You need to choose a focus based on your church's mission, gifts, and resources. Most initial church websites focus on potential attendees, attendees, and members. If you do choose to target people in vastly different groups, then you should consider creating more than one website. But choosing is critical; otherwise you and the visitors to your website will be confused.

Our main website targets potential attendees, attendees, and members. After the main website was up and running, we added two more websites. One supports our teaching church ministry and targets church leaders from other churches. The other is for our youth ministry and focuses on outreach to youth in our community. As you would expect, each of these three websites differs in appearance, content, organization, features, and website visitors.

What Do They Care About?

You have chosen the target audience(s) for your website. The next step is to determine what they care about. You may need to study your target audience(s) to better understand their needs; however, if you chose target audience(s) that you are already supporting, then you probably have a sense of what they seek.

When some churches start an internet ministry, there is a frantic push to put every existing church document online. The thought is that filling the website with content that already exists on paper saves time. This is probably not the best way to go about it. In fact, it could even be disrespectful to your visitors. Wisely choose the information you post to your website. Adding extra information in which people are not interested only clutters up the website and makes it more difficult for visitors to find the information they want. As a church, our mission is to serve people, and we can do so by providing relevant information. As you work through this process, you are likely to find that you need to modify some existing written information as well as create some brand-new information. The important thing is for the information to be something that website visitors care about.

Our mission is to serve people, and we can do so by providing relevant information.

You may want to use the following process, which worked well for us at Ginghamsburg. During one of the first meetings of the newly formed internet ministry team, hold a brainstorming session with a few leaders who serve in church communications. On a whiteboard, list each of the target audience(s). As a group, talk about and list the kinds of things you would want if you were a member of your target audience(s). If your target audience is potential attendees, think about viewing a website for a church you have never seen before—one you might want to attend in the future. What should be on that website to help you decide whether or not to attend? You might list things such as: directions to the church, what we believe, worship style, music style, worship times, pastor's biography, activities for kids and for youth, classes for adults, special support groups, current church activities, instructions for parking, instructions for dropping off a child, etc. Since this is a brainstorm, you will eventually need to refine and organize the list, but this will become the initial list of the content to gather or create for your website.

The next step, which can be done with the full group or a smaller group, is to go through each of the items on the list and discuss how to provide the content to the visitor. For example, "music style" might require more than a text description. Perhaps there is a non-copyrighted song you could post in audio or video so people can really get a feel for what your music ministry is like. If you have special parking for visitors, think about including a map or a photo to help visitors find it. Some churches create an entire sequence of pages that walk through a first visit to the church, telling visitors where to go, what they will see, and what they will do. For potential attendees, the first visit to a church can be a very scary thing. Starting with a virtual visit can make it a lot easier for them.

As you work through how best to provide content to website visitors, consider active features that can assist your target audience. For example, you may want to add a discussion forum, an e-mail newsletter, a calendar, a slideshow, forms, or a private area that requires a username and password. As with simple content, you should choose active features based on your target audience. There is more information on active features later in this book.

Go through the process of brainstorming, refining and organizing the content list. Decide the best ways to share the information on the website. Choose active features. Do this for each target audience you plan to support. Notice that the information you need may not be the same as the information that already exists on paper. For example, you may not have had a picture of the visitor parking spaces before. The key is to gather the right information for the people you want to serve, and present it in a way that makes sense to them. Once you know what the right content is, you can mobilize your team and church to gather and create it—whether text descriptions, photographs, audio, or video; and the technical member(s) of your team can begin to work on the active features.

The key is to gather the right information for the people you want to serve, and present it in a way that makes sense to them.

Now for a fun trivia question: Excluding the front page and other pages made up of mostly links and minimal content, what is the most-visited content page on the Ginghamsburg website? I have asked this question to church groups around the country, and only a couple of people have ever answered it correctly. The answer is at the end of the next section.

The Words We Use

In addition to choosing the right content for the audience, we need to choose the right words—ones that people can fully understand. Churches have a unique religious language. We use words such as "justification," "sanctification," "edification," "sacrament," and "holy." These church words may be unfamiliar or even intimidating for our target audience. Even the more common words such as "prayer," "communion," and "sermon" may be unfamiliar or may hold differing connotations for visitors with varied backgrounds. Especially in the more general and introductory portions of your website, use easily understandable terms or provide extra explanation to facilitate understanding. For example, instead of using the word "pray," use "speak to God through prayer" to provide additional explanation. Or you could refer to a "sermon" as the "pastor's message." The preferred language depends on your target audience and the words you use in your church. Church words are often important words for visitors and members to learn and understand at some point, but think carefully about when these words should be introduced, and start with words that the people you are serving are likely to understand.

We church people also like to create our own homegrown names for things. Our church uses various metaphors for children's ministry. Depending on the ages of the children, they go to "The Nursery," "The Tree House," "The Backyard," or "The Avenue." Classes can meet at the "MC," the "DC," or the "Arc." Within the church, these names are fun and come with a nice theme and logos, but to people in our target audience, they may be confusing. Easy ways to clarify terms are to add words that help define them ("The Avenue youth ministry") and to spell out acronyms ("Discipleship Center [DC]").

With any given target audience, writing for the internet is different than writing for paper. People are not typically willing to sit in front of a computer for long periods of time to read large amounts of text. The subcultures of the internet are fast-moving and to the point. People will read small blocks of potentially interesting text but quickly skip large blocks with a click of the mouse. So, existing written information may need to be adapted before you place it on your website. If at all possible, keep sections of text short and to the point. When in doubt, use fewer words.

Writing for the internet is different than writing for paper.

Some content, such as in an article or a sermon, requires more text. There are a few ways to make large blocks of text more likely to be read. You can provide a printable version. A printable version allows people to save hard copies and share them with others. You can also break up the text with section and paragraph titles, graphics, bulleted lists, and shorter paragraphs, or spread the text across a sequence of webpages instead of placing it all on one page.

Here is the answer to the trivia question at the end of the last section: The most-visited content page on the Ginghamsburg website is our pastor's biographical page. This is something we didn't anticipate. Perhaps this is because our pastor is well known, or because we have links to that page in several places. In any case, it seems reasonable that people will want to know about the pastor of the church. Your church website should include informative and personal biographies of your pastor and each of the main church staff.

Content Challenges

One tip to help your initial internet ministry days go more smoothly is to start your website with static content—content that is not changing all the time. For example, directions to your church and a description of what you believe probably do not change *Start your website with static content—content that is not changing all the time.* very often. In contrast, dynamic content is much more difficult to keep up-to-date. An example of dynamic content is a church calendar, which is best not posted at all if it cannot be kept up-to-date. Maintaining dynamic content makes it hard to build static pages because your team is frequently interrupted by the need to update the dynamic content. Dynamic content is best added when your team is well established and the church is committed to supplying the content to keep it going.

Another tip is to make gathering content a high priority. The number-one complaint I hear from people in internet ministry is that they are not able to get information from the church to populate the website or to keep it up-to-date. This can be frustrating for those responsible for the website and embarrassing for your church as website visitors see inaccurate or incomplete information. Perhaps an administrative person who is really connected with all that is going on at your church could be made responsible for getting the latest content to the internet team, or could be trained to make updates directly. At our church, we have had problems getting data from some ministry leaders for years. People who lead ministries tend to be busy people, and the internet is often the last thing on their to-do list. After years of frustration, we decided to change things. We still request information, but we post only what people give us. The ministries that give us information have great web-pages with lots of content. The ministries that do not give us information have a brief summary that we got from a previous brochure. As ministries see what is possible, they begin to want their section of the website to be better, and we receive more content. This has worked well for us.

Keeping It Legal

Internet ministry would be easier if there were no copyright, trade-mark, or privacy laws, but we must abide by them for both legal and moral reasons. You may have a wonderful recording of a song you want to post on your website, but you can't legally do so unless: 1) you own the lyrics and music, 2) you have permission from the owner to use the material, or 3) the lyrics and music are in the public domain. The same is true for musical arrangements. Old hymns are typically okay because they tend to be in the pub-lic domain, but you cannot legally post them if copyrighted arrangements were used to play them. You need permission to use both the words and the music. There are special licenses that you can purchase to sing and play music in your church, but unfortu-nately they do not apply to posting that same music on the internet. Most music licenses have some limitation on the distribu-tion, and the challenge with the internet is that it has almost infinite distribution potential. We post our sermons in streaming video; however, except for a few songs we wrote and arranged ourselves,

We must abide by copyright, trademark, and privacy laws for both legal and moral reasons.

we are not able to post the music even though we know it would be of great ben-efit. This becomes more of an issue when a sermon incorporates a song or a person speaks while a copyrighted song is playing in the background. The effect of speaking over music can be powerful. So for those times, we ask that the musicians use non-copyrighted music. A small portion of a song, especially when you cannot tell what song it might be, is allowed; otherwise, we must remove that section from the audio we post on the website.

Commercial video clips also have copyright issues. Portions of video clips from movies can be licensed for use inside a church worship service, but they are not allowed on the web at all, unless you can get permission. Experience has taught us that permission is either impossible to get or carries an outrageous cost. For this reason, we ask the pastor to summarize all clips from commercial movies or television before or after they play because the people who view sermons on the web will not be able to hear or see them. We remove all such clips from what we post online.

All website content is automatically copyrighted, even if there is no copyright notice on the website, so you need permission to copy content (text, graphics, audio, video, etc.) from another website. An e-mail granting permission is usually sufficient. You do not need permission to link to another website. In fact, most websites prefer the publicity because it increases their number of visitors and helps improve their search engine ratings.

Magazines, newspapers, photos, and other published material are typically copyrighted. You need to get permission from the owner and possibly pay a fee to use them. You can purchase photo and graphic libraries, which include permission in the license agreement for use on websites. There are also websites that claim to have copyright-free graphics, but it is difficult to know where they acquired all their images. Creating your own graphics is safest.

Original photos or video of non-copyrighted and non-trademarked items are generally okay to use on your website. If you take pictures of children, get written permission from their parents to use them on the web. It is good to have written permission from adults when using their images, as well. If you take pictures in public places where people cannot expect to have privacy, it is generally legal to post those pictures of adults.

Due to the various privacy laws and other issues, we often stage pictures that include only our staff or long-term church members and their families. We sometimes modify the photos to remove people or to obscure their faces. If anyone requests to have his or her picture removed from our website, we remove it immediately even when we have the legal right to use it. There is no reason to let conflict or discomfort continue.

It is best not to post personal phone numbers, addresses, or e-mail addresses on your website. For privacy, to avoid prank callers and e-mail spam, it is best not to post personal phone numbers, addresses, or e-mail addresses on your website. We ask people to call the church to get phone numbers or addresses. We set up automatic forwards so that e-mail sent to a church e-mail address is automatically forwarded to the person's private e-mail address.

These laws can be difficult to understand, but it is important for churches to follow them to avoid potential lawsuits and because churches should obey the law and treat people respectfully. I am not a lawyer and cannot give you legal advice. Please consult a lawyer for the details regarding these issues.

Help Them Find It

You may have a great plan for identifying and generating the right content and features, but the content and features won't serve their purpose unless the website visitor can find them. Organizing the website is very important. Most visitors understand that websites are organized into sections, subsections, and pages. Organize the content similar to the hierarchical outline of a book with chapters, sections, and paragraphs. The organization criteria should be something your target audience can understand.

Here is a way to get started: First, list the name of each piece of content you are planning to have on your website (pastor's bio, forum, directions to the church, etc.). Then, attempt to put the content elements into logical groups based on criteria that seem to make sense to your target audience. There should not be more than ten groups; five or six groups would be better. Once you are comfortable with the groups, they can become the major sections of your website. If you have many content elements in one group, consider splitting it into two groups or define subgroups.

Section names are important because they are key to a visitor having an idea of what is inside the section. Look at each group of content elements and attempt to name it with a word or a short phrase that the target audience will naturally understand. This can be very challenging, and there are

Look at each group of content elements and attempt to name it with a word or a short phrase that the target audience will naturally understand.

no perfect answers. Do the best you can. You may need to move content to a different group because it does not fit after you choose a section name. Avoid church words and local church lingo. At Ginghamsburg, for example, we should not have a section named "The Avenue," but a section called "Ministries" with a subsection called "Youth" might work well.

As you work through this process, you may feel the need to have sections, subsections, subsections of subsections, etc. To simplify access to the website content, try to minimize the "depth" of the website. The "depth" refers to the number of mouse clicks visitors must make to get to the content they seek. Keeping the depth to less than five clicks is usually best, and important content should not be more than a couple of mouse clicks away.

Here is an example of a website outline:

Home (front page)
About Us
    Services
    Directions
    What We Believe
    Our History
    Staff

News and Events
    Calendar
    News

Community
    Pastor's Blog
    Forum
    Prayer
    My Account

Ministries
> Adult
> Youth
> Children
> Missions
> Worship

Learn and Grow
> Sermons
> Devotional
> Classes

One option for choosing names is to make the section names action words, or verbs. Most visitors come to your website with a purpose. Action words more closely tie to the needs of the visitor. Here are some examples of verb-based section names: Worship with Us, Explore the Church, Meet Jesus, Grow in Christ, Connect with People, Serve Others, Get Support, and Nurture My Kids.

For popular pages that are a few mouse clicks into the website, you may want to create a "hot link." A "hot link" is a link, usually on the front page, that takes the visitor directly to a page inside the website. The page can be found through a sequence of mouse clicks, but the "hot link" bypasses all the normal navigation and takes the visitor straight to the page. A group of hot links on the front page is useful but not required.

Once you have a basic outline, test it! Gather a small test team. Pick content needs your visitors might have, and follow the process for finding that content. For example, imagine a visitor coming to the website for the first time. Imagine that this visitor has a thirteen-year-old son whom he or she wants involved in youth activities. Looking at the names of the sections and subsections, is this visitor likely to pick the right path through the website to get to the content he or she seeks? Again, this is challenging. Do the best you can.

The Most Important Word on Your Website

The most important "word" on your website is your web address because that is what visitors will type in and what other websites will link to. The most important part of your web address is your domain name, which looks something like this: *YourChurchName.org*. The domain name is the text that uniquely identifies your website among all other websites in the world. You may also hear people refer to your web address as a "URL," which is a techie term that stands for "Uniform Resource Locator." The URL includes a prefix that helps the computers know how to communicate. A full URL has the format: *http://www.YourChurchName.org*. Like the other content on your website, the domain name should be clear to your target audience. You want a name that people can remember and are likely to type in correctly, so you should generally avoid acronyms or abbreviations unless you are confident people will remember them. Pick a name that describes your website. For a church website, using your church name is usually best. The challenge is that all domains on the internet must be unique, so you may need to get creative in order to find a unique name. Including the word *church* in your domain name is optional. Shorter names are generally better, but they are more likely to be taken already.

You want a name that people can remember and are likely to type in correctly.

The letters in your domain after the dot ("dot" is web talk for the period symbol) are called the Top-Level Domain (TLD). The TLD is part of your unique domain name. YourChurchName.org is a different domain than YourChurchName.com or YourChurchName.us. Examples of TLDs are "com," "org," "net," and "info." It is best to register domains with both "org" and "com" as the TLD. "Org" was designed for non-profit organizations (like churches) and "com" was designed for companies. However, some people assume that "com" goes at the end of all domains, so it is wise to own both and to have either one take people to your website. There are no restrictions on who can register which TLDs, so it is fine for a church to register a "com" domain. The TLD can also be a country code. A country code is always two letters, and every country has a unique country code. The country code for the United States is "us." If "org" and "com" are not available for the domain you want to register, then you could use a country code. A few countries have interesting country codes with other meanings: Tuvalu has a country code of "tv," and Micronesia has a country code of "fm." Using a country code may cost more than other TLDs because the country to which they are assigned controls them.

Since the domain name must be unique, it must be registered. The organization that manages all the domains is called the "Internet Corporation for Assigned Names and Numbers" (ICANN), www.icann.org. ICANN does not sell domains, but there are many vendors and hosting companies where you can purchase a unique domain name. The typical cost is about $15 per year, and you can choose to purchase multiple years. Domain name vendors are easy to find with a quick web search.

Here are four pointers I hope will help you in the process:

1. Vendors often try to sell extras with your domain name, and it is unlikely that you will need anything except the domain name, so carefully skip past extra options.
2. Many hosting companies will purchase the domain for you. This solution will work if you trust the hosting company, if they are willing to put ownership in your name, and if they will provide you with login information to manage the domain settings yourself. I have worked with a few churches that decided to switch hosting companies only to discover that the hosting company they wanted to leave would not give them access to their domain settings or, worse yet, that the hosting company legally owned their domain. They could not move their website without a lot of conflict or possibly legal action. If you have ability to change your domain settings, then you have the option to move your website to a different hosting company at any time.
3. Your domain will be added to the ICANN database by any vendor with whom you register a domain. Domain name vendors can make the process a little easier for you by creating nicer web-based registration tools, but no company will result in a better registration.
4. If you register at one domain name vendor, you can transfer your domain name to another vendor if you would like. The process is not simple, but vendors are required to allow you to change.

Any vendor that offers domain names also has web forms that allow you to search for a new domain. You may see the term "whois" used to refer to searching in the database of registered domain names, which is sometimes called the "whois database." To find out if a domain is already registered, you type in the proposed domain and submit the form. I am always amazed at how many of the domains I attempt to find are already registered. Finding a unique domain name may take some patience. Just keep at it until you find one that will work for you.

Once you find a domain name that is not already registered, you can go through the registration process to purchase it and to enter its initial settings. You will be asked for contact information and for a list of your primary Domain Name Server (DNS) or, simply "Name Servers." You can get this list from your hosting company. The names vary but may look a little like this: *ns1.YourHostingCompany.net*. There will probably be three or more of them, and you need to list them all.

Domain names were created because people can remember text names more easily than they remember numbers; however, numbers work best for computers. The DNS does the translation from the letters in your domain name to a unique numeric identifier called an Internet Protocol (IP) address. The IP address is the unique number that corresponds to your web server computer on the internet. It is normally written down as four numbers (between 0 and 255) separated by dots. For example: 64.182.165.98. A primary DNS is one of a small number of DNS computers on the public internet that are designated as the official source for your domain name and the corresponding IP address. The primary DNS computers then share that information with DNS computers around the internet so people can access your website. When you register your domain, you must supply the list of primary DNS computer addresses as a way to get your website known to the internet. In addition, your web hosting company must add your domain information (domain name and IP address) to the primary DNS computers so they can share the information. Once all this is done, it usually takes less than forty-eight hours for the entire internet to know about your new domain. In fact, some computers are likely to know about it in just a few minutes. It really is amazing how well it usually works.

When you register your domain, you must supply the list of primary DNS computer addresses as a way to get your website known to the internet.

CHAPTER 4

WE WERE SURPRISED BY WHOM WE REACHED

Understanding the different people of the web

"This ministry is a Godsend for so many people. I know I'd personally be lost without it. Thanks for being there for me!"

A woman in Australia sends me an e-mail when our text sermons are running behind. She reads them, prints them, and selects the right ones for several different people she knows. Her ministry is to select and share sermons with others.

A soldier e-mailed me because the military computers did not allow him to install Real Video, so he could not watch our video sermons. That night, we began re-encoding the video in a format that he could watch, and we have continued to do so ever since. Another soldier, a military chaplain at a classified location wrote, "I enjoy checking out your website as I use sermons from the internet as commentaries in preparing my own sermons here in the field."

One Sunday while visiting my wife's family in rural Indiana, we went to the worship service at a small country church. Afterward, I shook hands with the pastor and told him we were visiting from Ohio, where we attend Ginghamsburg Church. He said that he visits the Ginghamsburg website all the time and, in fact, had used a couple of online sermons in preparation for the sermon I had just heard.

A woman in China pleaded with us to quickly fix a problem with our video sermons. "The sermons are a God lifeline for me. It is very difficult to get to the church in Shanghai, so we don't go very often. With the sermons being online, I can pull them up whenever I want to and listen to the messages. It's the next best thing to being in church."

A local TV news station interviewed a survival expert from our church who travels around the world, teaching soldiers how to survive if they get separated from their unit. On camera, he broke into tears as he talked about "pulling up" the sermons on our website to stay connected with the church and "to feel part of it again."

A man who is totally blind informed us that he browses our website all the time using a special program that reads the words on the page to him. Until he told us, we did not even know this was possible.

A church in Canada was without a pastor. They had no one to preach on Sunday. They contacted us and got permission to use sermons from our website. They printed the sermons and had someone in their church read them from the pulpit to fill in for the Sunday sermon.

A mother wrote, "This ministry is a Godsend for so many people. I know I'd personally be lost without it. Thanks for being there for me!"

A small group of young pastors-in-training who live in Kenya meets each week to study the Bible together. The Bible study they use is often downloaded from the Ginghamsburg website.

A soldier stationed in South Korea writes, "I am currently leading a women's study here at Camp Stanley and have recently been using the Bible study from the online sermons for our discussions. Your website is amazing and is ministering all over the world!"

A man who consistently listens to our video sermons was waiting in the hospital where his son was having surgery. A fearful mother was waiting there too and began to ask questions about God. The man told me that her questions matched a recent sermon he had heard on our website. He led her to the Lord by going through the main points from that sermon.

These are some of the more spectacular stories we have heard over several years of internet ministry. There is no way to know to whom your church website will minister. We never imagined that any of these people in these circumstances would come to our website. But we now know one thing: if we had not stepped out in faith and added the content to our website, then all these people would have missed a blessing.

But How Do They Find the Website?

People find websites in many different ways, and it is often difficult to determine exactly how or why. We know that many times plain old-fashioned word of mouth, or computer/internet-assisted word of mouth, is key. The internet makes the world so connected that it is now common and easy to send an e-mail to a friend and include a link to a website. Personal web logs, online discussion groups, articles, and other websites may link to your website. They all help people find you.

The first place to expand the reach of your website is right in your church. Once you have your website up and ready to go, you should include the church web address on all your publications. Wherever you include the phone number or physical address of your church, include the web address. Announce the web address in church and include it in the bulletin. Add it to your business cards. Add it to your church sign. Some churches purchase a huge banner with the web address on it and hang the banner on the side of their church. Most passersby will never enter your church; however, some may type in the web address from the banner just to see what it is all about.

The first place to expand the reach of your website is right in your church.

Search the internet to find places where your church website can be listed. Most denominational headquarters websites provide a place to list all the churches in that denomination, and the listings usually include a web address. People looking for a church may look to the denomination's website to find a church. There are also websites that serve local communities, and they will often list churches in the area. As a rule, we register at any website that appears to be reputable and lists churches. Think about where your target audience hangs out (physically or on the internet), and try to get your web address there.

Users can enter keywords on internet search engines such as Google and Yahoo!, and the search engines return a ranked list of webpages containing those keywords. (See chapter 8 for instructions about formatting pages to assist search engines.) First, you need to register your web address to help search engines find it. After talking to several churches and doing some research on my own, I do not recommend paying a company to submit your website to hundreds of internet search websites. The result can be that the e-mail address you provide ends up getting on e-mail spam lists. I recommend registering at Google, Yahoo!, and the Open Directory Project (www.dmoz.org). It is free, and will ensure that the search engines most people use will have your web address.

The Ultimate Information Source for Adults

Most people who did not grow up with the internet think of it as the ultimate information source—the largest and most automated library in the world. The internet is often their first or only source for any information they seek. I am glad that God makes all kinds of people because there is a fanatic about anything and everything, and they create great websites with great information. For example,

Most people who did not grow up with the internet think of it as the ultimate information source.

my mother has registered Bichon Frise dogs—cute, white, little fluff-balls. Before she got them, I had never heard of the Bichon Frise breed. I did a web search, and over two million pages came up on this one breed of dog. I am grateful for all the different kinds of people God created who are now creating websites and contributing to the ultimate information source.

The massive quantities of information on the internet have contributed to the internet culture's need for speed. The amount of information is overwhelming and growing at an increasing rate. So, adult visitors to your website are typically not going to spend much time systematically reading through everything. Instead, they will move quickly through your website in search of specific information. If they don't find it immediately, then they are likely to move on to another website. For this reason, it is important to have a well

Adult visitors to your website are typically not going to spend much time systematically reading through everything.

organized website that includes search capability. Local search gives visitors the ability to easily find pages by typing in a few keywords. If a visitor finds your website through a search engine or link from another website, then the first page he or she sees may not be the front page. It is important to have section and page titles to orient the visitor, and complete navigation on every single page. These are all ways to help adults quickly find the information they seek. Providing excellent content is the best way to keep them coming back.

Adults also like and use information-based active features. We have an online daily devotional, which includes a personal journal to store private notes and a public online community to discuss the devotional topics. Visitors often comment on the current topic and ask or respond to questions. Other features include a weekly poll about the sermon topic and a community prayer exchange that allows people to post prayer requests. Interactive features encourage visitors to go beyond acquiring information and begin to contribute and interact with others in community. As people interact online, there are additional opportunities to minister to them, and they are more likely to feel a connection to your website and church.

The Ultimate Cool Place for Youth

Youth, who have grown up with the internet, accept as common knowledge that it is the ultimate information source. From their perspective, the internet, with its vast sea of information, has always been there. Youth expect the information to be there, and they are unhappy if it is not. At our church, the comments we receive from adults are usually thanks for great content. The comments we hear from youth are often questions about why more information is not available.

To youth, the internet is less an information source than it is an active place where people go to do everything from hang out to play games to talk with friends. My teenage son summarized it well when I asked him why he does not go to our main church website. He said, "There is nothing to do there." That website has over four thousand pages that the adults seem to appreciate. It even has several active features, but from a youth perspective, "There is nothing to do there."

To youth, the internet is less an information source than it is an active place where people go to do everything from hang out to play games to talk with friends.

If you are a parent or a youth leader (I've done both and have the gray hairs to prove it), then you know that anyone who tells you they have figured out how to connect with youth is probably not telling you the whole truth. I don't claim to have figured out how to fully connect to youth via the web; however, I can share a few things that we have learned. Most of these are based on trial and error (heavy on the error part), and listening and observing.

First, unlike many adults who may not check personal e-mail for a week or two, most youth with internet access are online many times a day. They are web savvy. Computers and the internet way of doing things come naturally. So even if your website navigation and layout are not the best, youth will usually be able to find their way around. It is unfortunate that, in many cases, youth have few reasons to come to your website. Companies spend millions of dollars on websites designed to attract youth and ultimately to generate revenue from the online advertising or sales. The competition for the time youth spend on the web is fierce. Although youth are on the web frequently, they are probably not on church-related websites, even those targeted to them.

Second, youth want something to do. Instead of simply getting information, they want to post their thoughts, rate something, take a poll, find things, figure out a puzzle, play a game, get rewards or chances to win a prize, create something, or communicate with others. Websites for youth should be much more interactive than websites for adults. You don't need to add every feature, but you should consider how you can provide opportunities for interactive participation throughout the website.

Third, youth are multisensory and multitasking; they like music and other sound, video, and animation. My twin teenage boys often have multiple instant message boxes on the screen while they are playing a game, listening to music, and watching television—all at the same time. Youth are more adapted to processing multiple simultaneous stimuli; as a result, youth are likely to respond to sound and motion. Since your website is competing with several other things for their attention, you are best advised to create pages with less text and focus on the critical message you want to convey. Use links to take visitors to a detail page. I do not think youth have a problem focusing on one thing; instead, I

Youth are multisensory and multitasking; they like music and other sound, video, and animation.

think this is merely their way of adapting to the incredible amount of information and stimuli they receive. Once they identify something of interest, they can focus and go deeper.

Fourth, youth often have newer and better computers than the general population, and they are more likely to have high-speed internet access. This is not true everywhere, so you need to assess the youth you are serving. For us, knowing our audience has allowed us to add more media and interactivity. We sometimes add a video to the front page of our youth website. This is something we would never do on our main church website because people may not be able to play it.

So Where Are the Youth Going?

Clearly, youth are not flocking to church websites, but they are flocking to the web. Here are some of the popular things they are doing on the web:

Instant Messaging (IM)

IM enables two or more people to communicate live from their computers by typing messages back and forth. IM is talking by typing. Youth can spend hours messaging with their friends. I dislike typing because I am lousy at it. When I first tried IM, I remember thinking, "I can't believe any human being would like to communicate by typing." Now, I use it daily and really like it, even though I still dislike typing. IM has a way of growing on you once you get used to it and learn how "IMers" communicate. IM has an interesting lingo with abbreviations to ease typing ("lol" = laughing out loud, "brb" = be right back) and special symbols called emoticons that help express emotion (":-)" = smile and ";-)" = wink). Youth can instant message for long periods of time with multiple people, each communicating in a different window. They commonly type characters in all lowercase; all uppercase is considered rude and loud. The etiquette for starting and closing an online exchange over IM is different, too. Youth may not start with a greeting; instead, they may jump right into a discussion. There may also be long pauses in the discussion as they multi-task among other IM sessions and other activities. They may abruptly end the conversation without saying goodbye. They are not being rude; this is just the IM culture.

If you are ministering to youth, you should probably find out which IM service the youth in your area are using and get an account. I use a free program that accesses multiple IM services at once. I instant message with several youth around the United States, and from a ministry perspective I absolutely love it because these youth are more open to sharing how they are doing and to sharing spiritual things. I instant messaged with a middle school student off and on for over a year when he lost a close friend due to a car accident—tough stuff. The student told me how he felt, and we talked about the importance of following Christ now, because life is short. I was glad to be there to support him. Our conversation was probably more open and honest than it might have been if we had been face to face—I think he was crying as he typed. I also instant message with a young girl who has a mischievous streak. She is a smart Christian kid with strong morals and great potential for the future, but I bet parenting her is a challenge. She got in some sort of trouble at school—I never asked the details. She decided to hide it from her parents. I talked to her about the role of parents and the importance of telling her parents when she is having tough times, and she agreed. I like that ministering via IM can help youth right where they are right now.

If you are ministering to youth, you should probably find out which IM service the youth in your area are using and get an account.

In my experience, youth are more willing to share what they are thinking and feeling inside over IM than they are face-to-face. They are also more willing to listen to direct talk. IM is a powerful ministry tool. Face-to-face conversation and counseling will always be vital, especially for more serious issues, but IM creates an environment that makes communication a little easier and a little safer. It enables us to reach youth at different times and over great distances.

Personal Webpages

Another form of personal expression and communication for youth is a personal webpage. Free, public websites such as MySpace,

Xanga and Hi5 allow anyone to create a personal webpage. These services are usually supported by onscreen advertising. Page background, colors, fonts, pictures, music, etc. can all be customized. These websites are especially popular among youth and young adults. Web logs (also called "blogs") with entries from the page owner are among the most popular features. Web log entries are often made daily, like a diary. This is another place where youth tend to share a lot of very personal information, and in this case, that information is available to anyone on the internet. The personal webpage can be connected to other personal webpages via a list of friends, and friends can post to the pages of their friends. So, each personal webpage becomes connected in a social network of links among friends' personal webpages.

Personal webpages provide youth with the freedom to create and to express themselves publicly in a mostly non-supervised online world, and they also provide connection to friends and a feeling of belonging. Church websites will probably find it difficult to compete with systems like this because the network of friends would be much smaller and the content on the personal webpages would require constant supervision. However, churches can offer other website features that give youth the opportunity to be creative, to express themselves, and to connect with friends in community. Features like this are likely to make youth feel more connected to your church website.

Personal webpages provide youth with the freedom to create and to express themselves.

I offer a word of caution from our own experience as we began to use a personal webpage in our youth ministry. In conjunction with some of the more involved and mature youth at our church we went to one of these websites and created a personal webpage for our youth ministry—cool! The purposes were to connect with youth where they are, to promote our youth events, and to provide an online daily devotional. We created the personal webpage and quickly had 175 friends, each with links to those friends' personal webpages. That was exciting and encouraging. Then we learned some things that were not so exciting and encouraging. We found that when we went to the webpage, there were banner ads at the top. In general, the banner ads were not much of a problem, but occasionally there were banner ads that were much too sexually explicit for youth, or even Christian adults. This was not something we wanted to encourage youth to go to and see. We also followed the links to each of the 175 friends' pages to see what the personal webpages were like. Except for the occasional banner ad, most were great, even somewhat fun and creative. However, a handful of them included inappropriate photos, and some included significant amounts of profanity. We did some research and found that personal webpages attract sexual predators. We had to change our approach. Our first priority is to keep our youth safe, and there was no way to do that on these websites. Now, we don't encourage going there. We still have a page, but we changed our mindset from thinking of personal webpages as a fun place to seeing them as a somewhat dangerous mission field where youth hang out. The page now contains links back to our youth website, where we can ensure a safer environment.

Games

Games are another popular place for youth on the web. There are many game websites funded by advertising. The games can be rather sophisticated—ranging from card games to arcade-style games. Some of the games are multi-player, enabling youth to play with friends or random people who happen to want to play the game at the same time. Many games entail moving through levels and list the names of those who achieve a certain level. This can be a status symbol. Some games offer rewards for playing often or winning. These techniques entice youth to keep coming back over and over, and return visits generate more advertising revenue from advertisers targeting youth. Games tend to attract a younger audience, so the ads tend to contain less inappropriate adult content than those on personal webpages, but you still don't know who the advertisers will be.

It is unlikely that churches will be able to compete with the level of sophistication and quality of commercial online games. However, games add fun to a church website, and youth like to have fun. I sometimes feel that we Christians don't have enough fun and funny content on our websites. Being a Christian is a joyful thing. We joke. We laugh. We play. And it is good for youth to see that part of us. Try to create games that are personalized to your church. For example, include faces of your youth leaders or teachers. We did one where the kids could put silly hats and clothes on our senior pastor and the kids thought it was fun. Games are harder to produce, but they are a nice addition to a church website.

Games add fun to a church website, and youth like to have fun.

File Sharing

File sharing is another popular activity for youth on the web. File sharing requires special software on your computer that allows you to search for and download files from other computers on the internet. The files most often shared are audio or video files. The audio files tend to be music, and the video files tend to be music videos or movies. Almost all of these files are copyrighted and illegal to possess unless they are properly purchased.

Churches can help by occasionally providing audio or video to which they have rights or that are in the public domain. When music artists perform at our church, we often ask for permission to post their music and/or video on our website. Although the artists may be limited on what they can authorize, they sometimes allow us to post a song or a portion of a song; and that is a valuable addition to our church website. If the content is copyrighted, we add a notice that states that we have special permission to post it.

Blind Leading the Blind

When we started our internet ministry, we were surprised that people from other countries visited our website. But we were more surprised to find that people who are visually impaired regularly visit our website. We want to welcome and serve all people, and we had never considered making provisions for people who have special access needs. Worse yet, we learned that we were making browsing more difficult by the way we constructed the website. We really messed up and did not even know we were messing up. Greg, who attends our church, is totally blind. Greg described for me the special software that reads content and structure from webpages and uses speech synthesis so he can hear what is on those pages. Greg is a computer system administrator, so he operates his computer and browses the web all the time with the aid of this software. I am in awe of how God made us able to communicate in different ways. Whether we are typing to talk using instant messaging or we have a condition that reduces our ability to see, we adapt in amazing ways to continue to communicate.

Churches should lead the way in producing websites that are more accessible to all people.

The Web Accessibility Initiative (WAI, www.w3.org/WAI) is designed to help web developers create websites that are more accessible to everyone. Given the church's mission, I think churches should lead the way in producing websites that are more accessible to all people. Here are a few tips on how to make websites more accessible (Details are available on the w3.org website.):

Graphics and Photos

Graphics, including photos, need to include an "alternate" attribute and a "title" attribute that describe a graphic and its purpose. These attributes are placed in the HTML code for the page to associate a text description with the graphic. If you are using TYPO3 to create your website, the details of the HTML code are taken care of automatically, but you still need to remember to enter them when you add a graphic to a page. The special reader software can read them out loud to explain what the graphic is. The title attribute will also show up in a regular browser if users move the mouse pointer over a graphic. Both attributes are usually set to the same text.

Initially, we did not include these two attributes for each of our graphics, and the navigation for our website was done with graphic buttons that contained text in the graphic. The reader software can read text in the webpage but can't read text within an image. As a result, visitors using the special reader software had to guess at the meaning of our navigation buttons. The attributes would have helped by explaining the function of those graphics. We also used graphics to control the positioning of elements on the page. For example, we had an all-white spacer graphic that created space between columns of text. These graphics, which have no meaning, confused the users of the reader software as they tried to understand the content on the page. The reader had no way of knowing the graphics were only there for spacing. A website navigation button graphic looked just as significant as a white spacer graphic. Jesus said, "If one blind person leads another, both will fall into a pit" (Matthew 15:14). Well, we were blind to these details and clearly were falling "into the pit" and leading others there as well. Now, we try to avoid using graphics for spacing, and we include the attributes with all graphics and photos.

Video and Audio

All forms of media should include a description that identifies what the audio or video contains. If a transcription of the audio is available, a link to that transcription is helpful.

All forms of media should include a description that identifies what the audio or video contains.

If your target audience includes people who are hearing impaired, consider this. According to several of our church members who are deaf and who interpret for the deaf, many find it easier and more expressive to watch a person sign in American Sign Language (ASL) rather than read the text transcription. Sign language is easier for the hearing-impaired just as listening to the audio is easier for a hearing person. If you have interpreters who translate your worship service to sign language, then you may want to consider videotaping them and posting the video on your website. We tried this for a period of time by providing each week on our website ASL-interpreted sermons in streaming video. The video contained only the interpreter from the waist up. The deaf community appreciated these sermons. Websites for the deaf even linked to our website and praised our efforts. Unfortunately, we had technical problems with camera positioning and lighting that made the signing difficult to see, so we discontinued it. However, I continue to believe it is a good idea and encourage you to try it, especially if you have an active ministry for the deaf.

Hyperlinks

Hyperlinks allow the visitor to change to different pages by clicking on a link. It is not uncommon to have many hyperlinks on a page. People who are blind do not have the benefit of seeing the layout of the page and scanning quickly for links. Instead, they need to step through the page or tell the software to generate a list of all the links on the page. The challenge comes from hyperlinks that say things like "Click Here" or just ">>." The context of the page determines the destination of these hyperlinks. The context may be separated from the link due to the way the reader software processes and speaks the words on the page, so it is best to make hyperlinks that are more descriptive.

Make It Accessible

Accessibility is an important consideration for all people we serve. As we are able, we need to help website visitors who may have physical impairments that limit their ability to access a website. In addition, we need to support visitors with less capable computers and software and slower internet access. For example, most of the international people who are listed at the beginning of this chapter access our website over a telephone line using a modem. We need to be careful not to add features that exclude them. There are people with older computers who simply cannot afford better computers. We need the church website to work with less capable computers. One approach I really like is a Flash Player we use. The Flash video plays while the rest of the video file is being downloaded. In order to help ensure that the video can play while downloading, the player automatically measures the connection speed and selects one of two videos to play. One video is smaller and will play while downloading over a typical modem connection. The other video is larger and clearer but requires a high-speed connection. All visitors get the best that can be delivered to them.

> *We need to support visitors with less capable computers and software and slower internet access.*

Go to Them—the Internet Mission Field

Another option is to go to where the people are. In the past, churches have only dabbled in internet missions and evangelism; they have not really taken it too seriously. Perhaps the internet feels too different or they are not sure what to do. It is helpful to think of the internet as a mission field like any other mission field in the world.

If you were going to design the perfect mission field what would it be? I might describe it as...

...filled with millions of unsaved and accessible youth and young adults.

...a place where people openly, regularly, and publicly share their opinions, thoughts, feelings, concerns, fears, and needs without any prompting.

...a place where people connect with other people in community, and where people like and expect to meet new people.

...a place where many people provide a picture and a little information about themselves so you can know a little about them before you communicate with them.

...a place where it is okay to be creative, different, and simply yourself.

...a place where people openly debate, discuss, and exchange ideas, including spiritual matters.

...a place where people like to go and hang out—a place that is fun, sometimes silly, and where people smile and laugh.

...a place that is close to home so we can get there quickly when we have time, without immunizations, passports, or plane trips. And it would all be free.

...a safe place without danger or evil influences.

Except for the last characteristic, which can't happen in a fruitful mission field, this perfect mission field exists right now, down to every last detail. It exists on the internet in public online services that connect people in community: blogs, personal webpages, and discussion groups, including MySpace.com, Xanga.com, and others.

This perfect mission field exists right now, down to every last detail. It exists on the internet in public online services.

As you can see by the items on the list, public online services are a uniquely fertile and accessible mission field. Here are three ways they are like other mission fields. First, the internet has its own language, culture, and customs. "lol" means laughing out loud. It can also just mean that I acknowledge what you are saying. DID YOU KNOW THAT TYPING IN ALL CAPITAL LETTERS IS VERY RUDE AND CONSIDERED LOUD? In the online world it is. The online community can quickly spot an outsider, so as in other mission fields, it is important to learn the language, culture, and customs before you can be an effective missionary there.

Second, we must to go to them. Christians have tried to build evangelistic websites where people can come and meet Jesus. We have seen some small successes, but that is a bit like building a church in the suburbs and wondering why people from the inner city do not come. We can learn from mission ministry. As with other missions, we should identify, equip, and send missionaries into the places where the people are and can best be reached. We need to go to them.

Third, we need to recognize that the places on the internet where we are going as missionaries can be dangerous and filled with evil influences. I recently spent some time learning on my own how to be an internet missionary by visiting numerous personal home pages and following the links between them. During this time I saw more evil than I had seen on the internet in the last several years. As I thought and prayed about it, I became increasingly saddened by it all. So many people are lost, confused, hurting, and in need of Jesus. I challenge you, and myself, to begin evangelizing in this way. The time I spent learning was emotionally draining, but I know in my heart this is where we need to be.

As you plan and grow your internet ministry, I encourage you to consider sending out missionaries to the internet, using public online services. The mission field is plentiful. We just need to go.

CHAPTER 5

OUR FIRST DESIGN MISSED THE POINT

Embedding the church's DNA into the website look and feel

Every church wants its website to look great, and we did too. My first attempt at a design had those shimmering gold buttons that dominated the front page. Most of us agreed that the buttons looked great, even somewhat elegant. But something was wrong. The website just did not fit us. Ginghamsburg Church is located in a middle of a cornfield (sometimes it is a soybean field or a wheat field), and it is not close to any city. I would never describe us as elegant. We are very informal. People come as they are, and sometimes the pastor preaches while wearing blue jeans. I can't think of anything that is gold in our church, except the connectors on the audio cables. We don't have ornate stained glass windows or a big steeple. Our sanctuary feels more like a living room than the inside of a cathedral. My fancy gold buttons had to go—not because they were bad, but because they didn't fit our DNA.

The second front-page design was quite different and became the first design to go public. The design incorporated a stalk of wheat blowing in the wind with seeds leaving the stalk, and the colors were earth tones. We kept the buttons simple and placed them around the wheat. Designs have changed a lot since late 1996! I can't really say that any of our designs were good by today's standards; however, the design with which we went forward fit us, and it gave people a sense of what our church is like.

Finding Your DNA

What does your church look and feel like? I am not referring only to the physical building, which is a small part. I am referring to the personality and the atmosphere of your church. Are you formal or informal? Are you playful or serious? Are you an inner-city church, a suburban church, or a rural church? Are you traditional or contemporary? Are you multicultural? Are you big in missions? Are you gifted in the arts? Are you small and friendly? I love the diversity of God's creations. Churches are all made of groups of people, yet we are so vastly different. Churches are different in ritual, style, gifts, doctrine, and ministry focus; however, together we are the body of Christ. Life would be boring if not for all the diversity God created. It is okay to celebrate how God made our churches and us—each with unique DNA.

Having a website design that fits your church is important because the design is the very first thing visitors see. The design helps them understand what your church is about and what it feels like. Translating the characteristics of your church to a design may seem difficult and abstract. Here is one approach that has helped me: Start by browsing many websites. Assess whether they could match your church. Once you find a few that look like they might fit, combine the best design ideas to create your own design.

The design is the very first thing visitors see.

What Is in a Design?

The design of a website defines both its overall appearance and the way it operates. Because web design is the subject of full-length books and in-depth websites, this chapter will focus only on the basics and on the unique aspects of designing websites for churches. If you'd like more tips on church design, visit Great Church Websites at www.GreatChurchWebsites.org. The creator, David Gillaspey, has many tips on excellent design, and he has personally reviewed thousands of church designs. You can subscribe to see all the churches if you'd like, but the free features alone are valuable. Since design is often a matter of personal preference, please consider the following suggestions as guidelines rather than a strict set of rules.

The design layout defines the location of all elements on the page. Layouts often include across the top a banner graphic that contains the church name or logo in the upper left. A footer along the bottom works well for a copyright notice, church address, and contact information. On most websites, the main content is partitioned into one to four columns. We started with three columns—narrow columns on the left and right and a wide column in the middle. We liked that look, but over time it became harder to decide which content to place in which column. Now we use a two-column layout with the navigation on the left and the main content in a larger right column. For really wide content, such as forums or a calendar, we use a single column. It is okay to select a main column layout and then switch column layouts as needed to accommodate different types of content, as long as the pages look like they come from the same website.

The design also includes the supporting graphics, colors, and font styles. Supporting graphics can add features such as curves, lines, and shaded regions. They can also include photos and other images. Some churches like to have a picture of the church building on the front page or even part of the building design on all pages. That might be okay, especially if the building is distinct; however, the building usually does not tell much about your church's DNA. The church is the people, not the building! Because churches are all about people, it's nearly impossible to have too many pictures of people on a church website. As you think about banners at the tops of pages or pictures within the content, make sure there are pictures of people—people, people, people.

> *It's probably impossible to have too many pictures of people on a church website.*

Most churches want their website to be inviting and friendly. Lots of pictures of joyful people interacting with each other portray that feeling. Curved lines and gradually shaded regions work well because they seem less harsh. A white or light-colored background with open space around the content feels friendlier. Curved fonts, like Verdana, Arial, and Helvetica, are typically a little easier to read on a screen, especially as the text gets smaller. Textured backgrounds or backgrounds that don't contrast well with the font color can be hard to read and are therefore less inviting. A few years ago I was asked to review a church website with a bright red background and bright yellow text. I could barely read it. This is not welcoming to visitors. Inviting and friendly websites are pleasant to look at and read.

How Do I Drive this Thing?

Navigation provides the mechanism to move around to different pages on your website. The website should be organized into logical sections and subsections with pages in each. The navigation menu is usually located along the top or along the left side of each page. Top navigation frequently lists the main section names evenly spaced in a row. Left-side navigation usually lists pages within a section, in a vertical column similar to a shopping list. Left-side navigation can include the website section and subsection names as well. The advantages of left-side navigation are that it is intuitive, that it allows the visitor to see the list of links at all times, and that the vertical column can accommodate many links.

> *Navigation provides the mechanism to move around to different pages on your website.*

You can also use drop-down menus that display a list of links when a visitor moves the mouse pointer over a section name at the top of the page. You may not need both a drop-down menu and the left-side navigation. Drop-down menus make sense to most visitors because many computer programs use them, and they can save space on the page by eliminating the need for the left-side navigation. However, drop-down menus can be more technically challenging to implement across multiple browsers, and they can be more cumbersome for the visitor who must first move the mouse over the section name before seeing a list of pages. The approach you use for navigation is largely a matter of personal preference. We have tried multiple approaches on our different websites, and I have grown to prefer left-side navigation.

Another helpful website navigation feature is called "breadcrumbs." Breadcrumbs provide a visual indicator of where the current page is located in the depth of the website. Breadcrumbs usually look something like this: "Home > About Us > Staff" and are positioned near the top navigation. In this example, the current page is the "Staff" page, and it is in the "About Us" section of the website. The words in the breadcrumbs are links to pages at higher levels of the website. In this example, "About Us" goes to the "About Us" section page, and "Home" goes back to the front page. Breadcrumbs are not used often by visitors, but they can be handy to visitors who come to the website from a link on another website or from a search engine. The breadcrumbs give visitors a sense of where in the website hierarchy the current page is located. If you are using software that can automatically generate breadcrumbs, or if you have a large website, I suggest that you consider adding breadcrumbs to the design. (TYPO3 can automatically generate breadcrumbs.)

I mentioned that navigation is usually positioned along the top or along the left side of a page. Of course, navigation or content can be placed anywhere on a page, but as the web has evolved most websites have begun to use these general guidelines. By following these guidelines, you help your visitors to learn more quickly the method of navigation for your website. As much as possible, try to have navigation that is intuitive to your target audience. Navigation is a key method visitors will use to find the content on your website, so it is not the place to be tricky or overly creative. Nothing is more frustrating than a website with difficult navigation. Visitors may give up and leave.

Flash menus are an example of potentially frustrating navigation, so I do not recommend using Flash for navigation. You can use Flash to create beautiful cartoon-like animation with sound. From a technical perspective, Flash works well for creating fancy animated navigation. However, Flash menus behave differently than other approaches, and that can cause confusion. In addition, in order to run Flash navigation, the visitor must have the Flash plug-in installed before coming to your website. Also, the reader software used by the visually-impaired is likely to have difficulty interpreting Flash navigation. Chapter 7 provides more information on Flash and its uses.

We need to do our best to make it easy for visitors to use our website. To learn more about improving usability for your entire website, I recommend a book called *Don't Make Me Think: A Common Sense Approach to Web Usability,* written by Steve Krug (New Riders Press, 2000). This book helped open my eyes to a variety of usability issues. We want visitors to think less about how to operate the website and more about the content, since the content is where the ministry happens.

We want visitors to think less about how to operate the website and more about the content, since the content is where the ministry happens.

Just Pick One

You need to choose a design including the appearance and the navigation approach. I suggest that you visit many other websites for a test drive. You can visit other church internet ministries as well. Our children's ministry team likes to visit other churches that are doing children's ministry well. They learn by seeing other children's ministries in action. To visit a church, they need to arrange a time when they can meet, schedule a meeting, and travel to the other church. Visiting a church requires a lot of work. One thing that is unique about internet ministry is that you can visit any church internet ministry without ever leaving the comfort of your computer. Take advantage of this opportunity to learn from others. You can also visit commercial websites, which reflect the designs visitors are most used to seeing. Many popular commercial websites pay usability experts to make their websites as intuitive as possible, and they hire expert web designers to create them. We can look at them, learn from them, and implement the best ideas we see. We can't legally use their exact HTML code or graphics from their webpages, but we can learn and use ideas.

Visit commercial websites, which reflect the designs visitors are most used to seeing.

It is okay if you don't have team members with web design skills because many web tools come with templates. A website template is a set of files that define the appearance and navigation of a website. A template can automatically give your website a common look across all its pages. The Web-Empowered Church software comes with several professionally designed templates in different styles and colors. You can change the appearance and navigation of your website at any time by changing the template.

Once you pick a design, you should use it consistently across the entire website. When we first started our website, we tried to create a different design for each major section. We quickly found that each section felt like an entirely new website, and that was confusing for visitors. Of course, the design does not need to be exactly the same on every page. You can vary graphic elements or colors for different sections. That helps visitors identify the sections, and they will not be confused as long as the pages look consistent and operate in a similar way.

Don't be discouraged about not finding the perfect design for your church website. There is no perfect design, and there is no design that everyone will love. The time may come when you simply must choose. Just pick a design and know that you can change it as time goes on. Even the best design will need to be changed later for variety. And remember, the content remains the most important part of the website.

There is no perfect design, and there is no design that everyone will love.

CHAPTER 6

WE WERE LOST IN A BIG BOWL OF ALPHABET SOUP

Sorting out and understanding the internet ministry technology toolbox

First, there were acronyms: HTML, XHTML, CSS, XML, RSS, SQL, PHP, and CMS, just to name a few. Then there were "bumpy" words like JavaScript, then hyphenated words like e-mail and e-store, and then made-up words like podcast and cookies.

When we started learning about web technology tools, we felt like we were drowning in a big bowl of alphabet soup. It is difficult to learn something by reading if you can't understand the words you are reading! We were also surprised to learn that even the people who were using these words were not always sure what they stood for, but we needed to learn the language of the internet ministry tools we were using. Otherwise, we would not be able to understand statements like, "Podcast is really just RSS with an added enclosure tag," or, "Our CMS is written in PHP with a MySQL database." At first, it seemed impossible to get it all straight, but as we learned the lingo, we found that we began to talk funny, too.

This chapter and the next chapter are meant to be safe, guided tours of the terms and the tools in your internet ministry technology toolbox. This chapter discusses the fundamental tools that make your website go. The next chapter introduces you to multimedia power tools used for graphics, animation, sound, and video. For each technology tool, you will learn what it is, what it is good for, and suggested tool choices. This is not a survey of all tools—that would clutter both your mind and mine. Instead, I will try to focus on the tools you need to know and the essential information you need to know about them. You will also learn what the common buzzwords and acronyms mean—to keep you from drowning in the alphabet soup. In my experience, most technology is not as scary when you get past the terminology and understand what it does. You won't learn exactly how to implement each tool because that depth of information would not fit in this book; however, since these are the tools used by most internet developers, there are many books and online resources that can provide more details. Please fasten your seatbelt and enjoy this guided tour.

Web Browsers and Web Servers

Computers, modems, and computer networks existed prior to the development of what we know as the internet. Web browser and web server software made the internet possible and usable. A man named Tim Berners-Lee wrote the first web browser and web server in 1990. So, the very first internet ministry tool was created in 1990. After that, the internet grew slowly; the first church websites were probably not created until the mid to late 1990s. Most kinds of ministries in your church have been around for hundreds or even thousands of years, but internet ministry is just a baby—well, maybe a teenager!

Web browser and web server software made the internet possible and usable.

A web browser, such as Internet Explorer or Mozilla Firefox, is the software installed on your computer that allows you to access websites on the internet. When you type a web address into your web browser or when you click on a link on a webpage, the web browser communicates over the internet with the specific web server defined in the web address. The web address also designates a requested file and can pass some additional data. Web servers are computers on the internet running web server software. Web servers wait for requests from browsers. When a request comes in, the web server either gets the file from its hard drive or creates the file, and in the process the web server may also store some information. The web server then sends the file to the browser. A web browser may send multiple requests in order to get all the files associated with a webpage. For example, if there is a graphic on a webpage, the browser will process the page file and then see that a graphic file is needed. The web browser will then send out another request to the web server asking for the additional graphic file. Each one of these requests that a web browser sends to a web server is referred to as a "hit." You may hear website statistics that refer to "hits per day" or "hits per month." A "hit" is one request of the server.

A browser maintains a cache (pronounced "cash"). Cache is one of those technology words you will hear at different times. Caching is the storing of retrieved information that might be reused later; caching speeds the retrieval process. By storing the first copy of a retrieved file, the browser can just grab the locally-stored copy in the future instead of sending another request over the internet. This can save time. For example, let's say you have a common banner graphic on every page of your website. When a new user comes to the website, the browser will request the banner graphic file from the server; however, for future pages, the browser can just grab the banner graphic file from your local hard drive because the file is automatically stored in the browser cache.

As the browser receives the files or retrieves them from the local cache, it builds the view of a webpage from the contents of those files. The view is what you see as the webpage. A web browser's main function is to get files from web servers and to render (create the display of) pages. A web server's main function is to send requested files to browsers.

We can't control which browsers visitors use to view a website. This is one technology we can't pick. One of the challenges of building webpages is creating them in a way that can be rendered correctly by many different types of browsers. The next sections include tips on browser compatibility.

We can't control which browsers visitors use to view a website.

HTML and the Other Family Members

HTML stands for "HyperText Markup Language." HTML is the main language of the internet—it is what is used to create webpages. Don't worry about memorizing what HTML stands for; most people just call it HTML. The latest version of HTML is more accurately called XHTML, which stands for "eXtensible HTML." XHTML is the recommended modern-day language to create webpages. XHTML is a little more strict and specific than the old

HTML; therefore, different types of browsers render it more consistently. You will hear HTML and XHTML used interchangeably in normal web conversation, but just know that the XHTML specification is the one to use. The main specifications for most web languages are located on the World Wide Web Consortium (W3C) at www.w3.org.

HTML is the main language of the internet.

When a browser requests a webpage, the file that is returned contains HTML. If you look at the file, the file just contains characters. These characters tell the web browser how to render the page. The instructions for the web browsers are referred to as "tags." Tags are enclosed in less-than and greater-than signs. Here are some examples of common tags: <body>, <p>, <h1>, and <div>. Most tags have a start and an end tag. The end tag is indicated by a preceding forward slash, for example: </body>, </p>, </h1>, and </div>. A few tags do not have a separate end tag, so the slash is added to the end of the start tag, for example: <br/>. If you view a webpage file in a simple text editor, you will see text from the webpage intermingled with various tags that instruct the browser. There are many different tags with different sorts of instructions. How much you need to learn about HTML depends on how involved you are with the construction of webpages, but you will probably need to learn many of the HTML tags at some point. The good news is that modern day web editors write the HTML for you most of the time, so you don't need to rush out and learn all the details.

Lots of different browser-like programs are going to read your webpage HTML including multiple types of web browsers, special reader software for the visually impaired, and search engine programs. To maximize the likelihood that all these different programs will understand your webpages correctly, try to use valid XHTML on your website. The W3C has an online tool that can check your pages for you. You can automatically check a page for valid XHTML by using their Markup Validation Service at validator.w3.org. Most browsers will render a page, even with minor errors; however, the best and safest approach is to use correct XHTML.

Lots of different browser-like programs are going to read your webpage HTML.

XHTML is really part of the eXtensible Markup Language (XML) family of languages. XML is becoming increasingly popular, especially for storing or exchanging data. In XHTML, the tags are provided, but in XML you can define your own tags. The tags use the same format with less-than and greater-than signs. XML can tag any kind of data, and if a program writes information to an XML-formatted file, then another program that knows what the custom tags mean can read the information.

RSS and Podcasting

RSS stands for "Rich Site Summary" or "Really Simple Syndication." Like a lot of other web terms, many people who use the term RSS probably don't know what it stands for. RSS is also in the XML family of markup languages, so it has the familiarly formatted tags, but it has a specific set of tags used to define an index of items on a website. The purpose of RSS is to provide an up-to-date summary of available information on a website. That information is read by RSS reader software. Visitors can use websites that include online RSS readers or RSS reader programs on a local PC. The RSS readers retrieve designated RSS formatted files from one or more websites. The RSS reader uses the RSS files to provide the visitor with a quick summary of updated items on a website without requiring the visitor to browse the website. If the visitor wants more information, then he or she can click on a link and the web browser will go to the page on the website where the information is located. Initially, RSS was used largely for news feeds. Visitors can get a quick summary of the latest news stories and click on any that are of interest. Churches can use RSS for items like news, events, Bible studies, and sermons. Any popular list of items that changes over time can be included in what is called an "RSS feed." Tell visitors about the RSS feeds you offer by listing links to the RSS files on your website. Visitors need those links to tell the RSS reader software which RSS feeds to access.

The RSS reader uses the RSS files to provide the visitor with a quick summary of updated items on a website without requiring the visitor to browse the website.

RSS is a mechanism to help people manage and find the information they are looking for without browsing websites or sorting through large amounts of extraneous information. As we all experience information overload from the incredible quantity of information on the internet, mechanisms like RSS and the associated RSS reader programs become more popular. They are a nice feature for a church website.

To create an RSS feed that visitors can subscribe to, you need to create the special index file on your website and then keep it up-to-date. Creating the file manually can be challenging and prone to error. The best approach is to include software on your website that will automatically generate RSS files based upon updates for your website. Content management systems, such as TYPO3, can do this automatically for certain types of lists.

Podcast is a derivative of RSS and is used to distribute the latest versions of audio or video files. A podcast reader reads an index of the available audio or video files. Unlike RSS, the audio or video files are often automatically downloaded. If the visitor has an iPod or other portable media player, the files can be automatically downloaded to that player. The term "podcast" comes from combining the word "iPod" and the word "broadcast." But, a podcast does not send out a continuous signal like a broadcast does. Instead, the receiving computer actively requests the audio or video files from the server. From the web server's point of view, podcast files are not really special. They are simply files sent out in response to a web browser request, so you don't need any special web server software to podcast.

Podcasts work well for sermons or other periodic teachings. Since podcasts can be automatically downloaded, they are a way to make content more available and accessible. We have created audio podcasts of our sermons and a weekly Bible study for some time. People who use them tell us they like the podcast because it makes the content portable. For example, they can listen to a sermon while exercising, driving in the car, or traveling for business. For a church, podcasts are probably not going to be more popular than sermons posted on the website. However, if the sermons already exist in audio format, then all you need to provide a podcast is to create and maintain the podcast file itself and to tell people about it. After that, the podcast reader programs do all the work.

People like the podcast because it makes the content portable.

The podcast file is nearly identical to an RSS file except for an additional tag called an "enclosure tag." The enclosure tag provides information about the audio or video file including its location, size, and type. Since the files may be quite large, the included file size lets the program know the size before it downloads the file. As with RSS, you will benefit from automating the generation of the podcast file; it can be error prone and difficult to keep up-to-date.

CSS

CSS stands for "Cascading Style Sheets." CSS styles tell a web browser how to display HTML elements on your website. Prior to CSS, the format of the content was defined by format tags embedded in the HTML. This made maintenance very difficult. For example, if you wanted all your paragraph titles to be centered instead of left justified, you would need to go into each page in the website and make this change. This proved to be an inefficient approach because the formatting tags were repeated over and over in the pages. With CSS, a paragraph title tagged with a <H2> tag can be changed across the website by setting the CSS style for the H2 tag in common CSS file. In just one place, CSS tells the browser how to format the HTML elements throughout the website. And CSS styles define many features like location, alignment, background color, foreground color, spacing, borders, size, and fonts.

CSS tells the browser how to format the HTML elements throughout the website.

On our church website, we transitioned from the old embedded HTML format tags to the new world of CSS. It takes time to go through and remove the old tags, but the new pages are much easier to maintain, and they look better because CSS also provides style control that was never available with HTML format tags. We could not avoid this situation—CSS did not exist when we built most of the pages! The nature of technology is that it evolves. We must evolve with technology to get its benefits. We do not often enjoy change—we attempt to manage it—but change is not a surprise because it is just the nature of technology.

Unlike XHTML and RSS, CSS is not in the XML family of markup languages. (That was a lot of acronyms! If you mostly understood that sentence, you are learning techie talk.) CSS does not use XML tag formatting. Instead, a CSS file includes a list of the HTML elements with the settings for various attributes of the elements enclosed in curly braces, "{" and "}." The word "cascading" in "cascading style sheets" refers to the fact that styles defined first remain in effect within the page unless they are overridden with later style definitions. Also, styles applied to HTML elements are applied to HTML elements inside them. For example, the HTML body tag (<body> and </body>) must surround all the page content. If a style for the body tag includes a font attribute using this style rule: "body {font-family: times}" then the font "times" will be applied to all text on the page unless it is overridden by a style rule after the body tag. The styles cascade down through the HTML on the page.

Styles can be stored in a separate file or within the HTML. If you store the main styles for your website in a file, browsers can cache the file and reuse it to render other pages. A separate file eases maintenance because a change to one style will affect that style for all the pages on your website. Tools like the TYPO3 CMS can generate the CSS file automatically.

JavaScript

JavaScript is a scripting language embedded into the HTML to add interactivity to the webpage. There are other scripting languages, but JavaScript is the most popular and universal.

JavaScript is a scripting language embedded into the HTML to add interactivity to the webpage.

JavaScript is not Java. Although the two languages have some similarities, they have totally different functionality. The purpose of JavaScript is to add webpage functions such as dynamically changing HTML, responding to events like a mouse click, validating data entered into a web form, detecting the browser type, and creating or reading browser cookies.

"Cookie" is an unusual name for a mechanism that allows a webpage to write data to a small file on the visitor's computer. When the visitor returns to the website, the browser automatically sends the data in the cookie file to the web server. JavaScript or server software will react based on the data in the cookie. Cookies are commonly used to remember preferences or to automatically log on to a website. On our website, if a visitor logs on with a username and password and does not log out, we use cookies to automatically log the visitor back on during his or her next visit. In the past, there were privacy and security concerns associated with cookies. Although those concerns have been addressed, some people still disable cookies in their browser settings. So on pages we create, we cannot always count on cookies to be an available option because some people have disabled them.

JavaScript is a programming language, so it can be difficult to learn and understand. Fortunately, there are many examples of JavaScript on the internet, and these examples perform most common functions. There are lots of online resources that can teach you JavaScript.

JavaScript is either embedded into an HMTL page or placed in a separate file. The HTML "script" tag is used to tell the browser to interpret a section of the file as JavaScript instead of HTML. That tag looks like "<script type="text/javascript">" or just "<script>." The closing tag is "</script>." In most cases, it is not necessary to learn how to program in JavaScript, but it is an important part of web development since some page functions require it.

Server-Side Scripting

Server-side scripting is similar to JavaScript except that the script runs on the web server instead of within the browser. Server-side scripting is the programming used to dynamically generate pages for your website. For example, you may want to include a different Bible verse each day on the front page of your website. You would not want to store the Bible verse as part of a permanent webpage because you would need to manually change it every day. However, server-side scripting can read a verse from a file containing different verses and automatically change the verse for the day as part of generating the webpage. This is a very simple example. Server-side scripting can do many powerful functions, and the scripts can be quite large, even thousands of lines long. These scripts do all the processing needed to create your dynamic and interactive website.

Server-side scripting is the programming used to dynamically generate pages for your website.

There are many server-side scripting languages. The two most popular are Microsoft's Active Server Pages (ASP), which is more accurately referred to as "ASP.NET," and Personal Home Page (PHP), which is an open source solution. These two server-side scripting systems are both popular and full-featured. Either one is a good choice.

ASP.NET is commercial software from Microsoft. It is a good choice if your church is a heavy user of advanced Microsoft software or if there are people on your team who already know ASP.NET. As commercial software, ASP.NET has the advantage of additional documentation, training, and technical support. You will need to set up a Microsoft Windows server to run ASP.NET, so you will probably pay more than you would with open source software because the Windows Server software is fairly expensive. Also, in my experience, ASP.NET may require more web-server-computer memory and processing power. ASP.NET is popular for use on large corporate websites.

Unlike ASP.NET, PHP is licensed as open source software, and that license gives you the right to use the software and modify it without paying for it. The original authors retain copyright ownership of the software, so you cannot sell it or remove copyright notices from it. Besides being free, another advantage of open source software is that anyone can get the software-source-code files used to create the program. Most people simply use the software and don't work with the source code, but having the source code allows you the option of modifying or enhancing the software. If you modify the software, then you can use it freely and can also submit the modifications to the open source project for possible incorporation into a future official release of the software. In this way, the community of users can contribute to making the software better. Open source software is often developed by people with varied skills and motivations who contribute to the project without being directly paid for their work, so the quality may vary substantially. In general, the quality and documentation for commercial software is more consistent than that of open source software. PHP is a large and popular open source project, so the quality and documentation for PHP are excellent. And, it is free too!

Open source software matches the way many churches think and operate. Most churches are concerned about keeping costs down, and open source software provides significant capabilities at no cost. Moreover, churches encourage people with different skills and gifts to join in community to work together and volunteer time, which is how open source software is created and maintained. Church communities often give freely and substantially for the common good and the benefit of others. And, of course, open source software is given for free. I am not saying that there is any sort of divine connection to open source, but I do think that open source makes sense to Christians and that we should seriously consider this option for acquiring software within churches.

Open source software matches the way many churches think and operate.

Because it is open source, PHP is developed by a community of actual users who are focused on an excellent server-side scripting system for creating webpages. The result is that PHP is popular, full-featured, and tailored for web development. One measure of PHP's popularity is the website HotScripts.com, which provides scripts you can use on your website. HotScripts currently lists over twice as many PHP scripts as scripts in any other language. While it is unlikely you will use most of these scripts, they are an indicator of the popularity of PHP.

Both ASP.NET and PHP are good choices; however, I recommend PHP due to its capabilities, popularity, and reduced web server software costs. Also, PHP is the scripting language used to write the TYPO3 software. Thanks to tools like TYPO3, you will probably need to know very little server-side scripting. If you need to learn PHP, there are many books available, and php.net is a good reference.

Databases

Databases store and retrieve information on a website. Server-side scripting generates the pages, but databases manage the website data. For example, a database can store a list of events in a church calendar. Each event could include a date, title, and description. By using the event data in the database, server-side scripting can generate a page that lists the next ten church events or a page that displays the current month's calendar. Website visitors see up-to-date information because these pages change automatically as events change and as time passes. As websites become increasingly automated and interactive, the need for databases increases. In fact, since databases add such flexibility, the trend is to store most website content in a database. This has been common for commercial websites for years.

Databases require separate database software running on your web server. Microsoft SQL Server is an example of a commercial database program. MySQL is a popular example of an open source database program. There are many other database programs as well. A database program is installed and available as part of a typical web server computer. The acronym "SQL," which is used in database program names, stands for "Structured Query Language." Most people refer to it by the letters "S-Q-L" or pronounce it like the word *sequel*. SQL is the common language programmers use to command the database software to perform functions such as storing and retrieving data. Server-side scripting sends a command called a "query" to the database server. The database software stores data in a combination of special internal files and computer memory, and returns data to the server-side scripting in response to a query. For example, when constructing a church calendar, a query could request all calendar events for the current month. This information would then be returned to the server-side scripting for use on a webpage.

The database software stores data in a combination of special internal files and computer memory, and returns data to the server-side scripting in response to a query.

A database is a group of data defined by a database name and protected with a username and password. Database software may store many different databases. A database is divided into tables, each with a unique table name. A table is a list of similar data, such as a calendar-events table or a registered-website-visitor table. Each table is made up of individual records. A record is one element in a table, such one calendar-event record or one registered-website-visitor record. Records are made up of multiple fields. Database software supports different types of fields for storing different types of data such as date, number, and text fields.

For example, a database might have a table named "Events," which contains one record for each stored event. Each event record might have three fields: event date, event title, and event description. This simple database table structure can support a church-event system that could store, retrieve, and display many church events.

Content Management System (CMS)

A Content Management System (CMS) is comprised of a combination of server-side scripting, data files, and a database. These are all installed and run on a web server connected to the public internet. A CMS is usually large in terms of the number of files, disk space, required memory, and required processing power. Commercial CMS packages can be very expensive. Traditionally, only large companies have been able to afford a CMS, but changes in technology and the arrival of open source versions like TYPO3 have helped make CMS software more commonly available.

As the name indicates, a CMS is a system to manage the content for websites. A CMS stores content in files and database tables and then uses the stored information to dynamically generate webpages. A CMS allows you to create and maintain a website and to add interactive features. TYPO3 and some other CMS packages have special administrative webpages that allow you to create a website using a standard web browser on your personal computer. With a proper username and password, you can make updates to your website from any computer connected to the internet. In fact, multiple people can help maintain your website, even at the same time.

A CMS is a system to manage the content for websites.

Besides being a handy way to develop and maintain a website, a CMS has some other useful features. With a CMS, the look and feel of the website is separated from the content. "Look and feel" refers to the overall appearance of your website (look) and the way the website operates, including navigation (feel). The CMS accomplishes this separation by using templates. As mentioned in chapter 5, templates are a series of files, including CSS, and settings that define the website look and feel. Templates define characteristics such as layout, banners, curves, lines, buttons, navigation, menus, sidebars, breadcrumbs, headers, footers, colors, and fonts. One powerful feature of templates is that they take care of formatting automatically so that you can enter content without manually adding the website-wide formatting. Before we started using TYPO3, we had to manually set fonts and other formatting as we entered the content. That made both content entry and maintenance more challenging. Templates allow you to change the entire look and feel of your website in seconds, giving it a fresh look while preserving all the content.

Templates allow you to change the entire look and feel of your website in seconds.

Another unique feature of a CMS, and TYPO3 in particular, is database-driven dynamic content display. For any page or for the content on any page, you can set a start date for it to appear and an end date for it to disappear. The content is then displayed only during the specified range of dates. We often use this feature to keep the website automatically up-to-date. During one summer we had many camps, so we created a page that listed and described each of the camps. By appropriately setting the correct end dates for every camp, we managed the information automatically. Each camp disappeared from the page the day after it was over. The day after the last camp, the entire page disappeared from our website. This was all automatic once we set the dates. Some churches switch to a CMS for this feature alone. The content elements that automatically disappear from a website are not deleted; they are simply hidden from the public. You can reuse them by updating the content and adjusting the dates.

In addition to setting start and end dates, you can use dynamic content display to limit access to a page (or specific content within a page) to a particular set of visitors. Visitors log on by using their usernames and passwords, and they see different content based on what they are authorized to access. We use this feature for sections of the website limited to church staff, certain leaders, or various other groups. This powerful tool enables volunteers to access from anywhere special information that helps them serve the church. For example, our music team can privately post the schedule for weekends and events, along with the planned song titles, but only the music team members can access this information.

I strongly encourage you to use a CMS to assist in creating your internet ministry. The alternative is to create individual pages that are posted on your website. The non-CMS approach works for small websites, but as your web ministry grows, as you want more people to help update the website, and as your website becomes more community-based and interactive, a CMS will quickly become essential. Today, most any significant commercial website uses a CMS. Churches should have those same benefits.

Use a CMS to assist in creating your internet ministry.

There are so many choices for CMS software that the choices become confusing. Even the definition of CMS is blurred by product claims. I have looked at many but don't keep up with them all because of time constraints. From our experience, I recommend that you use the TYPO3 CMS. If your website uses TYPO3, the Web-Empowered Church ministry provides many additional resources (like this book), church ministry features, and a world-wide community of Christian TYPO3 users. The last chapter will provide more detail on the Web-Empowered Church ministry.

CHAPTER 7

WE TRIPPED WHILE TRYING TO MAKE THE WEBSITE DANCE

Using multimedia power tools

When I set out to build our first webpage, I decided to add a custom graphic. Adding a graphic to a page seemed pretty straightforward. I created a simple graphic. That wasn't too difficult; in fact, it was even fun. However, when I tried to save the graphic, the program I was using offered me a choice of thirty-one different file formats in which to save, including many options I had never seen before. I had a one in thirty-one (or 3.2 percent) chance of guessing the right one. Options are supposed to be good, but they don't feel good when you don't have any clue which one to pick.

Words are nice, but graphics, animation, sound, and video can make a website dance. As we continued on the journey to build Ginghamsburg.org, it seemed like each technical feature we added to the website resulted in another time-consuming investigation to figure out what technologies were available, what they could do, which one we should use, and how to use it. We call these investigations *adventures* because each one seemed to be a somewhat painful exploration filled with unexpected twists and turns and dead-ends.

Once I figured out the right graphics file format to use and got some pages working, we decided to add videos of our weekly sermons. Oh, no—another adventure! We learned that some video formats must be downloaded before they will play. Other formats can download and play at the same time. Some won't play on some computers. Some require an uncommon browser plug-in. Some require special server software that we could not afford. And none of them did everything right. There are many cool technologies to use on your website, but the adventure of understanding them and deciding which ones to use can be unpleasant.

This chapter continues the safe, guided tour with an overview of media power tools. If the tools in the previous chapter are the tools that make your website go, then these are the tools that make your website dance. This is not a survey of all power tools. Again I will try to focus on the tools you need to know and the essential information you need to know about them. Once again, fasten your seatbelt for the guided tour. This is the fun part!

Graphics

Photographs, cartoons, and other images add to the appearance and communication of a website. Some of the main web graphic file formats are Graphics Interchange Format (GIF), Joint Photographic Experts Group (JPG), and Portable Network Graphics (PNG). Each can display any graphic, but the file size and the quality of the resulting image may vary substantially. It is best to save graphics in the default file format that your graphics program uses.

Some of the main web graphic file formats are Graphics Interchange Format (GIF), Joint Photographic Experts Group (JPG), and Portable Network Graphics (PNG).

These source files will probably be much larger than JPGs, GIFs, or PNGs, and they will not display on the web, but using the default format makes it easier to modify the graphic in the future and ensures the graphics retain their maximum quality. When you are ready to put a graphic on your website, you can save it to a web-compatible format.

GIF: A GIF-formatted graphic can contain 256, 16, or 2 distinct colors in its color palette. A graphic is made up of a series of dots often referred to as "pixels," and the color palette contains the list of all colors used in the graphic. Each pixel is set to one color in the color palette. In order to reduce the file size required to store the color palette and the many pixel colors, GIF files are compressed. The GIF compression method is lossless, which means that the final image displayed is not altered by the compression process. For very simple images made up of just a few colors, reducing the color palette to sixteen colors can substantially shrink the file size. Due to the limited color palette, GIFs work best for cartoon-like graphics that use few colors or when large regions of the graphic contain one solid color. Logos and buttons usually work well in GIF format. These types of graphics should display with good quality, and the file size should be lower.

GIF also supports setting one of the colors in the color palette to transparent, which means that any pixels set to the transparent color will not be filled. The transparent pixels will display whatever colors are behind the graphic. For example, if the background color of your website is white, the transparent pixels will display the color white, but if the background color changes to black, then those same transparent pixels will display the color black.

GIFs work best for cartoon-like graphics that use few colors or when large regions of the graphic contain one solid color.

One of the fun aspects of GIF graphics is that you can animate them, which is a feature not found in JPG and PNG graphics. To animate a GIF, you create a sequence of individual GIF graphics and combine them into one file with your graphics program. Each graphic is a frame in the animation sequence. The animation sequence is controlled by setting the time delay between frames and setting whether the sequence loops through the frames forever or stops at the last frame. The final animated GIF file size is the total of the size of each of the frames in the sequence. The files can get large very quickly, so it is important to minimize the number of frames.

The thing to remember with GIF-formatted graphics is that the color palette is small; when you save a graphic to GIF format, the graphics program will select colors to fill the palette. If you have too many colors in your image, the program will change them and may use a technique called "dithering." With dithering, pixels that are side by side are set to colors in the palette that produce the desired color if the two colors are combined. For example, a light blue region of color might be filled with alternating dark blue and white pixels. The result is something close to the original image, but it may look a bit grainy or textured. Dithering is a common technique and can be seen by looking very closely at your television screen. From a distance, it looks clear, but very close it looks like a mess of different colors.

Currently, we can freely use GIF graphic files. Previously, Unisys Corporation and IBM Corporation owned patents on the GIF format.

However, it appears that the last GIF software patent expired by October 2006.

PNG: Previously, in response to concern that Unisys or IBM might force everyone to start paying to use the GIF format, a new graphics format called PNG was created. PNG stands for "Portable Network Graphics" and is an open standard. You can use PNG graphics in place of GIF graphics, but there are a few differences. The PNG format supports millions of colors, while GIF format supports only up to 256. Like GIF compression, PNG compression is lossless, but PNG compression usually produces smaller files than GIF compression. PNG graphics support transparency, but some browsers do not properly display PNG transparency. PNG graphics do not support animation.

JPG: The JPG format supports millions of colors—16,777,216 colors to be exact—and high levels of compression. Unlike GIF and PNG compression, JPG compression is lossy and can be adjusted. Raising the compression factor reduces both the quality of the graphic and the file size. JPG graphics also include an option called "progressive encoding" which allows a graphic to display before it is completely downloaded. Initially the image is somewhat unclear, but the detail fills in as the remainder of the graphic is downloaded. JPG graphics do not support transparency or animation.

The JPG format is perfect for photographs. Photographs are substantially smaller in JPG format than in GIF or PNG. The quality of the photographic image usually looks better than it does in GIF format because the JPG format supports so many colors. We commonly set the JPG compression factor to about 10 percent, and the difference between the original graphic and the final JPG is nearly undetectable if you look at the two images side by side.

The JPG format is perfect for photographs.

If you are unsure about compression settings or whether or not to use JPG, GIF, or PNG, use your graphics program to save the file to multiple formats and then compare file sizes and appearance. The quality of the image and the resulting file size vary substantially due to the content of the graphic. Sometimes you need to experiment and then pick the best one. Of course, the smaller files are, the faster they will download to a website visitor.

Browser Plug-ins

Plug-ins are separate software that visitors download and install to add features to a browser. For example, a plug-in can enable a video to play in a webpage or a formatted document to display inside the browser. The challenge with relying on plug-ins is that visitors may not have them installed, may not feel comfortable installing them, or may not be able to install them. Unless a plug-in provides an important feature, it is best to require only common plug-ins that are most likely to be installed and ready to run on your visitors' computers. Below are a few common plug-ins that I do not recommend.

It is best to require only common plug-ins that are most likely to be installed and ready to run on your visitors' computers.

Java Applets: Java applets are small programs that can run inside a browser. The issue with Java is that some visitors may have Java disabled because of rumors of security issues. Also, Java is quite large to download and somewhat sluggish when it runs. Part of the sluggishness is caused by the fact that Java applets can be large and can take time to initialize and run. So, in most cases, it is probably best to stay away from Java.

ActiveX: ActiveX is similar to Java. As with Java, you can develop powerful applications that run as ActiveX controls. However, based on browser security settings, ActiveX may be disabled, or a visitor may need to click on a warning message before the ActiveX control can download. The biggest issue with ActiveX is that it is a Microsoft technology that will not work in some browsers, or may work only after installing special plug-ins. For these reasons, it is probably better to avoid using ActiveX.

Flash

Flash was developed by Macromedia, a company that was purchased by Adobe Systems Incorporated. Flash is a powerful and versatile multimedia technology that supports animation, interactivity, audio, and video. Flash applications are often referred to as "Flash movies." Flash movies are surprisingly small considering the amount of media they contain. Flash is one of the most commonly installed and used plug-ins. Using Flash movies is fairly straightforward, but creating

Flash is a powerful and versatile multimedia technology that supports animation, interactivity, audio, and video.

Flash movies is hard. The challenges with creating a custom Flash include the cost of purchasing commercial Flash development software and the technical challenge of learning and developing Flash. Custom Flash development is a special skill among web developers. Fortunately, you do not need to own the development software or be a Flash developer to use existing Flash movies on a website.

On church websites, Flash has many possibilities. For example, Flash works well for interactive games and animated teaching or story-telling. We use Flash for multimedia e-cards—web-based greeting cards that visitors can select, personalize, and send to others by e-mail. The resulting e-cards, which are displayed in a webpage, include animation and music. The e-cards can be quite beautiful and emotionally moving.

Some churches like Flash so well that they choose to do their entire website with Flash. I strongly discourage you from doing this because it can be very difficult to maintain. In addition, the navigation and behavior of the website are often not intuitive to visitors and are unreadable by search engines.

PDF

PDF stands for "Portable Document Format." PDF is a popular file format for creating electronic versions of paper documents. You can use PDF-generation software to print a complex document to a PDF file (instead of a printer), and the resulting electronic document file will look almost exactly like the paper document. The PDF file retains all the original document fonts, graphics, and formatting. If you upload PDF files to your website, visitors have the option of downloading the PDF file and printing it. The free Adobe Reader plug-in is required to view and print the PDF document, but this plug-in is very common, so most people should have it.

PDF files are ideal when you want to post a highly formatted document to a website so people can download and print the document file. Our church student-ministry permission forms are an excellent application for PDF files. Completed permission forms are a requirement for students to attend youth events, and these forms must be printed out in order for the parents to sign them. PDF files work well for forms that require signatures.

PDF files are ideal when you want to post a highly formatted document to a website so people can download and print the document file.

Many churches use PDF files too often because PDF files are easy to create from existing files that are intended to be paper documents. If you have a document stored on your computer and you print it to a PDF file, then you quickly have something to post on your website. Unfortunately, PDF files are not well suited for online reading because most people prefer not to read PDF files on a computer screen; PDF files can be slow to download; and the PDF plug-in works differently than most website navigation. Also, when visitors click on a link to a PDF, they may feel like they've left the website.

If your visitors need to read information online, it is usually best to post the content on standard webpages. Having said that, there may be times when you should post content in PDF format. Some paper documents are long and have a great deal of formatting. For example, our "Events and Classes" brochure is quite long and packed with specially formatted information. We choose to post it in PDF because it would take an incredible amount of time to extract the information from the brochure to post it online, and people tend to read the paper version anyway. So, the electronic copy in PDF format is an easy way to provide a backup copy for anyone who needs it. The same is true with our weekly bulletin. It is highly formatted, and everyone in church already gets a paper copy. We choose to post the weekly bulletin in PDF format as well.

A printable webpage is an alternative to a PDF and can work exceptionally well in most cases. A printable webpage is specially styled with a template designed to support printing to paper instead of viewing online. Typically, banners and other webpage-specific formatting are removed or minimized to make the page look cleaner and to prepare it for printing. A printable page is still a standard webpage. We use this technique for most of our content that is likely to be printed, such as text sermons and Bible studies. We like this approach because: 1) with the help of the CMS, the same content

A printable webpage is an alternative to a PDF and can work exceptionally well in most cases.

can be automatically used to display both online pages and print-able pages; 2) with modern CSS styling, the printed document can be close to the quality of a PDF document when it is printed; 3) the printable webpage is more easily read online, and some people prefer to read that version; and 4) printing a printable webpage does not require any plug-in; the visitor merely prints the page from the browser.

Audio

Compared to other audio formats, such as WAV, MP3 file sizes tend to be smaller for the same audio quality.

In the past, there have been many competing audio file formats to use for web audio; however, the MP3 file format is now most popular. MP3 stands for "Motion Picture Experts Group Audio Layer 3." Compared to other audio formats, such as WAV, MP3 file sizes tend to be smaller for the same audio quality. This, plus the popularity of portable MP3 players, has contributed to widespread use of the MP3.

One challenge with placing audio files on your website is that the files tend to be larger than other web files. If you store a lot of audio files, running out of disk space on your server may become an issue. However, the bigger issue is usually the time it takes visitors who are connected to the internet via a telephone line and a modem to download these files. A thirty-minute sermon typically results in a 7.2 megabyte MP3 file, which takes about thirty minutes to download for a dial-up visitor. Waiting thirty minutes would disappoint visitors who want to listen immediately to the sermon.

Progressive download is a technique that allows an audio or video file to play while it is downloading normally from a web server.

Progressive download is a technique that allows an audio or video file to play while it is downloading normally from a web server. A browser plug-in downloads a portion of the beginning of the file first and stores it in the computer's memory. This is called "buffering." Then, the file starts playing from the beginning of the file. The file plays as the download process continues simultaneously.

As long as the downloaded portion of the file stays ahead of the portion of the file that is playing, the file will continue to play to the end without pausing. With a common modem connection, a visitor can listen to an entire thirty-minute sermon after waiting about twenty seconds to begin. If the download cannot keep up, then the player will pause for a few seconds to allow more of the file to download into the buffer, and then it will continue playing.

Another approach related to progressive download is called "streaming." People often refer to progressive download as streaming; however, the two are not quite the same. Streaming requires a streaming server—a web server with additional streaming software that orchestrates the download of media content. A streaming server communicates with a plug-in in a browser and attempts to maximize the quality over the current connection. The advantage of streaming is that downloaded data can be dynamically adjusted prior to the file playing and as it plays. For example, if the connection starts out fast but then slows down for some reason, the software on the streaming server can automatically reduce the amount of data sent. This reduces the quality but can allow the stream to continue without pausing. For video, a streaming server may continue to send the same audio stream but remove many of the frames of the video. So the audio plays normally, but the display appears jerky due to the missing frames. Of course, frames can be added and quality can be improved if the connection improves. Streaming servers can also support jumping into a latter part of the file quickly without downloading the first part of the file. Another advantage of streaming is that streaming software often supports live streaming. Like live television, live streaming is transmitting audio or video as it is captured. With live streaming, one computer usually captures audio or video and sends it to the streaming server on the public internet. The streaming server then sends the live stream out to visitors shortly after it is received.

For the majority of churches, I do not recommend live streaming. Because the internet has an on-demand culture, visitors are seldom willing to figure out time-zone differences and visit your website at a specific time in order to see a live event. A better solution is to record a version that can be posted shortly after the event and can remain on the website for visitors to access at any time. Additionally, in most cases, church events contain some copyrighted material such as music. Even copyrighted material acceptable for use in a church setting is usually not allowed on the internet. You must remove this material—a fairly easy task if you prerecord and edit the media, but a much more difficult task if you immediately send the event out on a live stream. With a live stream, you must edit and replace copyrighted material as the event is happening. Finally, live streaming requires highly reliable equipment and internet connectivity. At our church, our internet connectivity goes down occasionally, but since we choose to record events, we always have the option of taking the final file somewhere else to upload it to our web server (which is located at a hosting company).

A streaming server has a few nice features; however, a streaming server can be expensive to purchase and set up, the number of simultaneous streams to visitors may be limited, and visitors need a browser plug-in. Also, many churches host their websites in a way that makes streaming impossible or cost prohibitive. A better alternative is a full-featured progressive download approach with which any church website can include audio in most any hosting situation.

A better alternative to streaming is a full-featured progressive download approach.

For MP3, I recommend three mechanisms for delivery. First, use a free Flash MP3 player (available from Web-Empowered Church) that supports progressive download. Since it is Flash, no additional plug-in is required. With progressive download, visitors will hear an MP3 file start to play shortly after they click the play button. Second, provide a link to the MP3 file so the visitor can download it to play later or to manually copy to a portable MP3 player. Clicking on the link can also cause the MP3 to play inside whatever MP3 player program a visitor has on his or her computer. Place the Flash MP3 player and the download link near to each other so visitors can choose. Third, consider adding the MP3 file to a podcast. One huge advantage of using MP3 is that the same files can be used for progressive download as well as for downloading and playing.

Video

As with audio, there are many video formats from which to choose. The most popular video formats used on websites include Audio

Video Interleave (AVI), Motion Picture Experts Group (MPEG), RealMedia (RM), QuickTime (MOV), Windows Media Video (WMV), and Flash Video (FLV). Based on the video capture/editor software you are using, your initial video files will probably be in AVI, WMF, MPEG, or MOV format. As with graphics, you should initially store the video files in the common format used by your video capture program to maintain quality and to facilitate modifying them in the future. Also, each video file format has its own special mathematical technique, or "codec" (coder/decoder), for compressing video. Converting video from one codec to another can result in loss of quality due to interference between the codecs. It is best to stay with one main format while you edit and then convert it to the final web format when you are ready to post the video on the web. There are a few acceptable formats for web video, but I believe that FLV is currently the best choice for adding video to your website and MPEG-4 is the best choice for video podcasting. What follows is some basic information about these common formats.

> *FLV is currently the best choice for adding video to your website.*

AVI: AVI is a common capture format, so your files may start as AVI files. AVI files are often very large and may not play on all computers because of different codecs required to view them. AVI is not recommended for posting on a website.

MPEG: MPEG-1, MPEG-2, and MPEG-4 are usually too large for viewing with streaming or progressive download. MPEG-4 in particular is a popular and recommended format for video podcasting. Video podcasting is implemented like audio podcasting but uses MPEG-4 video files instead of MP3 audio files. In general, video podcasts are less popular than audio podcasts, probably because video podcasting is newer; the video files can be quite large to transfer and store; and many portable media players cannot display video. However, video podcasting is worth considering, especially if your church is already media savvy.

RM: RM, which stands for "RealMedia," was a dominant web video format for several years. The RealNetworks Helix streaming server that streams RM files is expensive but supports true full-featured streaming, and the plug-in can support progressive download as well. Most of our older sermon video is encoded as RM files.

Unfortunately, over the past few years we have received numerous complaints from visitors about both the RealPlayer plug-in used to view the video and the RealNetworks company website itself. Each visitor must manually install the plug-in, and during installation if visitors are not careful to select the right options, the RealNetworks software will become their default viewer for several common audio and video formats. They may also inadvertently agree to frequent e-mails from RealNetworks. Once installed, the plug-in produces more pop-ups and messages than it should. In short, visitors find it annoying. In addition, RealNetworks occasionally has sexually suggestive advertising on the front page and advertises inappropriate video services. Even though visitors were only directed to the RealNetworks website to download the plug-in, we are not encoding in RM format anymore, and I do not recommend it.

MOV: MOV is Apple Computer's QuickTime format. Quicktime can support streaming or progressive download. It is also sometimes used for video podcasting. As expected, QuickTime works well on a Macintosh computer. For Windows users, the biggest challenge with QuickTime is that the download installation file for the QuickTime plug-in is quite large, over 20 megabytes. People with dial-up connections find it difficult to download; they sometimes just give up. Also, like the RealPlayer plug-in, the QuickTime plug-in can be intrusive by setting itself as a default player and generating too many informational pop-ups. I do not recommend using the MOV format.

WMV: WMV is Microsoft's video format. For Microsoft Windows users it is preinstalled and works well. Getting and installing plug-ins for non-Microsoft-based computers is challenging. The plug-ins are now free but must be installed, and they are not always kept up-to-date. WMV supports streaming, and the streaming server comes with the latest version of Microsoft Windows server software. The Windows server software is fairly expensive, but it supports video streaming, including live streaming. One key advantage of WMV is that, if your computers are already running Windows, then you have the basic tools you need to edit and produce video. Due to the popularity of Windows and the availability of the tools, I consider WMV the second-best solution. And if you specifically need live streaming, WMV is probably the least expensive solution.

FLV: FLV is a newer web video format. The FLV format can support both streaming and progressive download. In order to stream FLV video, you will need the Adobe/Macromedia streaming server. Like most other streaming servers, it is fairly expensive. The biggest advantage of the FLV format is that it can play inside a webpage using the popular Flash browser plug-in. The way FLV files play is a little different from other video formats, because other video plug-ins usually only play video. But Flash is more general purpose and supports animation, audio, and video. A Flash movie plays the FLV, and the Flash movie is like any other common Flash movie, except that it includes Flash-provided features to do progressive downloading and to play an FLV file. This different way of playing video opens up some interesting possibilities. For example, you could develop a custom Flash movie that is the FLV player for your website. Or you could embed the FLV within a Flash animation sequence. In other words, you can display the FLV anywhere and at any point in the Flash movie.

Of course, you do not need to create Flash movies in order to create and play FLV files. Several free Flash movie FLV players are already available. If you use one, make sure it supports progressive downloading—not all of them do. The Web-Empowered Church has a Flash movie that will play FLV files. The player supports progressive download and has a unique feature that measures each visitor's connection speed and then automatically selects one of two Flash video files to send to his or her browser. One FLV file is encoded for modem connections and therefore displays fairly small, usually about 160 pixels by 120 pixels. The other FLV file is encoded for high-speed internet connections and usually displays in 320 pixels by 240 pixels. With this Flash movie FLV player, visitors will automatically receive the FLV optimized for their connection speed. Automatically selecting a video file based upon a visitor's connection speed is a feature normally only available with streaming servers. While this feature does not make all the dynamic changes that an actual streaming server can, it does make this important adjustment at the start of the connection. It also allows the visitor to manually choose which video to play.

With this Flash movie FLV player, visitors will automatically receive the FLV optimized for their connection speed.

As you work with FLV files, note that since FLV files require a Flash movie to play them, they may not play on your local computer when you click on them. If this happens, you can search for "Stand-alone FLV Player" on the web to find, download, and install a free stand-alone FLV player.

As with MP3 files, you may want to offer visitors the option to download FLVs by providing links directly to the FLV files. Using these links, visitors can download and save FLVs on their computers, and play them any time using a stand-alone FLV player. This is a useful option for visitors with slow or intermittent connectivity to the internet.

As you can see, the big advantage of selecting Flash as a universal plug-in to support animation, audio, and video is that visitors need only one main plug-in. And that plug-in is one of the most popular of all plug-ins. Over the years we have endured the challenges of multiple special and changing plug-ins. It was not pleasant at times, and the options will probably change again! However, we are currently pleased with this approach, and I expect that you will be as well.

The big advantage of selecting Flash as a universal plug-in to support animation, audio, and video is that visitors need only one main plug-in.

CHAPTER 8

WE FOUND LOTS OF UNEXPECTED CHALLENGES ALONG THE WAY

Tips on creating and maintaining your website

I remember when we created our thousandth webpage. What an achievement! Within a few months, some of the staff suggested we do a complete redesign of the website. What a great idea! Little did we know how much work that would entail.

When our CyberMinistry had been going for three years, the entire team was still made up of unpaid servants. We had at least one thousand HTML files because we had not yet reached the era of CMS (content management software) and database publishing. We had hundreds of graphics files and a few hundred video and audio files. When the staff from our church came to me and suggested that we do a redesign to give our website a fresh look and feel, I agreed that this was a great idea. Of course, there was one minor detail. Okay, it was a major detail. The complete look and feel of our website was stored over and over in each of the one thousand HTML files. In each file, we faithfully reproduced the banner across the top, the footer along the bottom, the buttons in the button bar, the copyright notice, the paragraph title styles, the fonts...everything. And, worse yet, most of the pages were created by hand, so even though they looked the same, the underlying HTML was often surprisingly different. The inconsistencies made writing programs that could read these files and automatically change the look and feel more difficult.

To this day, we are recovering from many of our past decisions as we continue to update and enhance our website at an increasing pace. We have certainly had our share of mistakes along the way. In this chapter I will share what we have found to be the best practices for creating and maintaining an excellent church website. These practices come from our experience and from the experiences of friends engaged in internet ministry at various churches. We have not figured it all out; what I share is simply the best of what we have learned so far. We are always learning and growing, and that makes internet ministry fun! Speaking of fun, here are a few slogans I wrote to express some universal feelings:

- If you think you understand computers, then sit back and enjoy the brief moment.
- Computers are here to humble us, not to help us.
- I look forward to the day when a computer will make something easier.

We Need a Heavenly Website Host

Before you look for a place to host your website, know what your hosting needs are. Start by choosing a Content Management System (CMS), because a CMS often has specific hosting requirements and you can quickly rule out options that would not support your CMS. Next, identify special features you need, such as supporting many

Start by choosing a Content Management System (CMS), because a CMS often has specific hosting requirements.

e-mail accounts or serving many large audio or video files. Fortunately, most packages that can host a CMS come with the other features you will need. Finally, as you compare packages, be sure to look for the frequency of backups. A backup is a copy of your data made to a tape or another hard drive; it is used to recover from a hard-drive failure or an accidental file or data deletion. Nightly backups are best.

Web-Hosting Application Service Providers (ASPs): Some CMS software is available only from specific web-hosting Application Service Providers (ASPs). "ASP" refers to a mode of business in which the ASP organization supplies online services that allow remote use of special ASP-owned software running on ASP-owned computers. Web-hosting ASPs can be ministries or commercial companies, so costs can range from no cost to quite expensive. Web-hosting ASPs run their own custom CMS, and users do not have access to the CMS software. Most web-hosting ASPs provide packages that include their CMS and various other hosting options such as e-mail and data backups. If you choose a CMS from a web-hosting ASP, you have automatically selected your hosting arrangement. Some churches like this because many of the details are handled for them. Also, web-hosting ASPs commonly provide an array of website templates and can usually develop custom templates for a fee. Some specialize in hosting church websites and provide special features that churches need. Most advertise themselves as easy to use, and many live up to that claim. Using a web-hosting ASP is a way to get your church on the web with a profes-sional-looking website very quickly. Web-hosting ASPs are a quick and easy way to handle the technical details of getting your church on the internet. If you plan to use a web-hosting ASP, consider the following suggestions:

Web-hosting ASPs run their own custom CMS, and users do not have access to the CMS software.

1. Sometimes these services limit the growth of your web ministry. For example, you may want to add interactive features, databases, e-mail lists, audio, or video. Be sure the web-hosting ASP has adequate growth options. Pay attention to limitations of all types such as bandwidth, disk space, numbers of accounts, and numbers of pages.

2. Adding features such as increasing network capacity and disk space can be expensive relative to the initial package. Verify that growth options are affordable.

3. Think about how you might move your website content to a different hosting arrangement in the future. Even if the web-hosting ASP provides great service, it is unlikely that you will host with them forever. Things change. People change. Financial situations change. Organizations come and go and merge with others. Moving a website can be painful. Since you will not have access to the CMS software owned by the ASP, find out if they have any methods of extracting the content from your website to help you move it to a new location. These methods are not common, and the usual solution is to

spend many hours manually copying the content and files to your new location.

4. Look for copyrighted features such as templates or graphics. Also look for proprietary applications to which the ASP may claim intellectual property rights. If you move your website in the future, you cannot take these with you unless you get permission from the ASP, and permission may be impossible or costly.

I have worked with a few churches that chose to use web-hosting ASPs and had beautiful templates. They used the templates for years, and the website look became their church brand. When they decided to move their website, they learned that the template they used was copyrighted and could not be used elsewhere. It felt like their template was being held for ransom; and they were very upset about it. But because the ASP owned the template, there was nothing they could do except create a new template at their new location.

Web-hosting ASPs are not evil. They typically have huge investments in their custom CMS software and the other features they provide. They need to protect that investment to stay in business. They also help churches because they offer a fast and easy way to get started. You need to understand the relationship and choose based upon your own needs.

Commercial and Open Source CMS: There are numerous choices for commercial and open source CMS software. It is not possible to list and compare them all here because there are so many and they change so frequently, but you can find more information by searching the web. Some of the things we considered when approaching this decision for the Web-Empowered Church are: God's provision, content entry, multilingual capacity, dynamic content, extension installation, templates, hosting options, cost, powerful capability, and extensive support. Based on these, we chose TYPO3 as our CMS. For an explanation of how TYPO3 addresses each of these criteria, please see chapter 11.

When considering non-ASP solutions, once you choose a CMS that appears to meet your needs, you can look at its hosting requirements. Server requirements may be listed as Windows,

WAMP, or LAMP. If the CMS requires ASP.NET server-side scripting, the web server should be a standard Windows server running the Microsoft Windows Server operating system, Internet Information Server (IIS) web server, and SQL Server database. WAMP-configured servers run the Windows operating system, an Apache web server, a MySQL database, and PHP (which is usually included in Apache). Notice that the first letters from each software component spell out the word "WAMP." The LAMP configuration is like the WAMP configuration, but the operating system is Linux instead of Windows. TYPO3 installs and runs best on LAMP- or WAMP-configured servers. There will also be requirements for memory and disk space. As a rule of thumb, more memory is always better, and disk space is not generally an issue because disk drives are usually large. Hosting details can be a bit confusing. If you are unsure about requirements or features, ask your prospective hosting company.

Once you know the configuration of your server, there are some additional options to consider. You can choose to host your website on either a shared server or a dedicated server. A shared server hosts many websites on the same computer, but a dedicated server hosts only your church website. For most churches, a shared server, also known as "shared hosting," is a good choice. Shared hosting is less expensive, and most church websites do not need all the resources of a dedicated server. In general, most websites are hosted on shared servers, and most web-hosting ASPs offer only shared hosting. In the early years of the Ginghamsburg internet ministry, our website was on a shared server, and it worked well for us. We later moved to a dedicated server because of increased disk-space requirements caused by years of stored sermon video.

You can choose to host your website on either a shared server or a dedicated server.

One potential issue with shared hosting is that the hosting company may put too many websites on one server, which can result in sluggish performance or memory errors. In addition, it is possible for any of the websites on the server to run scripts that slow the entire server down. The quality of service of shared hosting can vary but is not typically a significant issue. If you are unsure, begin with shared hosting because you can always move to a dedicated server later. A dedicated server is nicer if the increased cost is not an issue.

Self-hosting is also an option. With self-hosting, you host your website on a computer at your church or in someone's home or perhaps a local small business. The challenge with this approach is providing reliable service to your visitors. Visitors expect a website to be accessible twenty-four hours per day, so it is important to host where the internet connectivity is extremely reliable and where backup power is available. Most hosting companies have multiple redundant connections to the internet to reduce network outages, and they have backup generators that keep computers running when electrical power fails. Also, most hosting companies provide additional services such as monitoring the networks for hacker activity, 24/7 support, creating backups, and making security updates. These services can be time-consuming to perform, and they often require special expertise. Unless you have unique hosting capabilities, it is usually best to host with a fully equipped hosting company instead of self-hosting. Due to network reliability concerns and costs, we have never seriously considered self-hosting our church websites.

It is usually best to host with a fully equipped hosting company instead of self-hosting.

Choosing a hosting company is difficult. There are many options, and until you make a choice you don't know the quality and service that you will ultimately receive. Here are a few items to consider when choosing a hosting company:

1. **Free Hosting**: We greatly appreciate ministries that provide free hosting to churches. They have paved the way for more churches to get online. However, if you want to truly web-empower your church ministries, you are likely to quickly outgrow these hosting services. Many of them are not able to host a CMS like TYPO3 because it uses too many web-server resources; and they must host and support many websites at a very low cost.

2. **Paid Hosting**: It is probably not a good idea to use hosting packages that cost $5 or less per month unless they are subsidized in some way. Five dollars per month is not

enough income to cover the costs for the server and support or to ensure that the server is not overloaded. Excellent shared hosting is worth at least $1 per day, or about $30 per month. As your church becomes web-empowered, your website will likely more than pay for itself through reduced paper and mailing costs. Try not to make cost the dominant deciding factor when you choose a hosting company.

3. **Ask for Advice**: As with other services, it is helpful to ask people where they host their websites and if they are pleased. Larger hosting companies can often provide more features at a lower cost, but service can be limited. Local hosting companies can provide personal service. You need to shop for a hosting company and find a hosting package that fits your needs. You always have the option to move to another hosting company at a later date.

The Ginghamsburg Church websites and the Web-Empowered Church websites are hosted at VineHosting.com. Vine Hosting and the Web-Empowered Church ministry are ministries of the Foundation for Evangelism, so hosting your church or ministry website at Vine Hosting indirectly helps the Web-Empowered Church ministry. Vine Hosting will install TYPO3 and the Web-Empowered Church software for you for free so you can get started very quickly.

Hosting your church or ministry website at Vine Hosting indirectly helps the Web-Empowered Church ministry.

It Is Free, but...

As churches, we try to keep costs down. One way we sometimes try to cut costs is to use free commercial online services such as blogs, personal webpages, and mailing lists. Perhaps you could create most of your church internet ministry this way. These services are paid for with advertising on the webpages and in the e-mails they send out. Most people understand that the ads pay for the service, and that is fine. Unfortunately, we typically have no control over what is advertised. From personal experience, we know that these ads are not always the kinds of ads we would want associated with our churches. As we all know, at times advertising can be sexually explicit or otherwise inappropriate.

There are two main issues at hand. First, a church needs to be a safe space for the people we serve—a place where people can feel safe and trust, a place where people can heal and recover. So let's say we set up a free e-mail list to send out e-mails to everyone in the church. Setting up the list is easy, and now we can electronically send the church newsletter. One of the recipients is a new church attendee who is battling a sexual addiction and has been previously jailed for sexual assault. He began attending church again to get his life back together. The church sends out a mass e-mail that he reads from top to bottom, since it came from the church. At the very bottom of the e-mail is a somewhat suggestive ad with a link to a website that sells women's lingerie. It is not pornographic or illegal, but

A church needs to be a safe space for the people we serve.

to a person battling a sexual addition, this could be a temptation or worse. We can't take chances that our church message will be hijacked for commercial purposes. The church needs to be a safe place.

Second, many visitors assume that the church endorses whatever is on a church-sponsored website, including ads and links to other websites. For years we linked to the RealNetworks website to help visitors find and download the RealPlayer video plug-in. One day we learned that RealNetworks was advertising a streaming video version of a popular pornographic magazine on the page to which we were sending visitors. This upset many peo-

Visitors will assume we endorse the websites to which the links take them.

ple, even though we have no control over what RealNetworks puts on their website. We now rarely link from our website to other websites because we know that we will need to monitor the links and that visitors will assume we endorse the websites to which the links take them.

Development Tools

Which tools you use to develop your website depend on personal preference and the computer you are using. Most of your team should not need to purchase anything. There are links to many popular tools on the website for this book. The types of tools you may need include:

Browsers: It is important to have multiple popular web browsers on your computer to test pages and ensure that they display correctly in different browsers. Examples: Internet Explorer and Mozilla Firefox.

HTML/CSS Editor: In the past, a "what-you-see-is-what-you-get" (WYSIWYG) editor was the most critical tool for anyone creating websites. These editors help develop HTML, CSS, and JavaScript. Most people who use a CMS will not need a WYSIWYG editor to create pages. I used a WYSIWYG editor almost daily for several years. With CMS, I can go for several months without using one. WYSIWYG editors remain useful tools for advanced web developers, template designers, and server-side-scripting developers. Example: Dreamweaver.

Programmer's Text Editor: All computers come with a basic text file editor installed, but website developers commonly use more powerful text editors that include features like tabs for editing multiple files at a time, color highlighting of tags and keywords, and advanced "find and replace" features. Getting a programmer's text editor is optional, and you can add this tool at any time. Examples: NoteTab Light, Codewrite, and UltraEdit.

Graphics Editor: A basic graphics editor is an important program for most web developers. The key features include cropping, resizing, adjusting color and brightness, and saving in the JPG or GIF format. All computers come with a basic graphics file editor installed, and these tools may serve the need. Serious graphics designers, however, need much more capable graphics editors. Examples: Paint Shop Pro and PhotoShop.

> *A basic graphics editor is an important program for most web developers.*

Audio/Video Editor/Encoder/Player: If you plan to include audio or video on your website, you will need software (and possibly hardware) to capture and edit the audio or video. Depending on the software you are using to capture and edit, you may need additional software to encode files into different formats. You may also need an audio or video player. Some or all of these tools are likely to be already available on your computer. For most church web applications, you will need only basic editing tools, but the features you need depend on your capability and the output you desire. Examples: Movie Maker and Premiere.

Flash: If you plan to edit or create Flash movies, you will need Adobe (Macromedia) Flash. It is not required if you only plan to use Flash movies or Flash video. Example: Flash.

Word Processing: Website content commonly arrives in a Microsoft Word file, so it is usually important to have word processing capability to extract the content. Example: Word and Open Office.

Spellcheck: A spellcheck that can check the spelling of fields in a web form is a very useful tool, especially when a CMS supports entry of content into web forms. Example: Google Tool Bar.

File Transfer and Remote Shell: In most cases, your website administrators will need tools to securely log on to your web server and to transfer files. Some of these tools may already be on your computer. Examples: Putty, Remote Desktop, and WS FTP.

E-mail, Instant Messenger: You will want to communicate among web-team members. Two useful tools are e-mail and Instant Messenger. Again, it is likely that you already have these on your computer for other reasons. Examples: Outlook, Eudora, and Trillian.

Don't Create a Mess

Before you get started with your developmental tools, it is important to do some planning. Even for a simple website, the files and directories can quickly become a mess. When we started putting our sermons online in text format, we created a folder called "sermon" to store the sermon graphics. Each weekly sermon had about eight graphics associated with it. After a year and a half, the folder contained over five hundred graphics files, which made listing the files very sluggish. We realized that we could not have just one sermon folder for all graphics because it would end up with thousands of files in it. We now have one sermon folder per year. We also came up with a way to name our sermon graphics files based on the date of the Sunday that they were preached. The names looked like this: "apr1097a.jpg," "apr1097b.jpg," and "dec1497a.jpg." In order to ensure that you can find files on your growing website, have at least a general plan for where to store different files. The plan needs to be something that makes sense to all the people creating your website. We base most folder names on the names of the sections of the website. For example, we have an "About Us" section on our website, so we have an "aboutus" folder where we store files associated with the "About Us" section. The "aboutus" folder has a subfolder called "staff," where the staff pictures are stored. This approach makes sense to our team. For periodically generated files like sermons and newsletters, we add the year to the end of the folder name. For example, we have folders "sermon00" and "sermon01" for sermon files for the years 2000 and 2001, respectively. Filenames can also become confusing unless they have some consistency. For files associated with a date—like a monthly newsletter, audio sermon, or the weekly bulletin—include the date in the filename. For example, you could use the format "YYYYMMDD" where YYYY is the year, MM is the two-digit number of the month (with a leading "0" if needed), and "DD" is the two-digit day (with leading "0" if needed). Following this format, "b20070128.pdf" or "bulletin012807.pdf" could be the weekly bulletin file for January 28, 2007. The advantage of this approach is that the files sort chronologically and it is easy to find a file for any specific week. Our experience has shown that most files are associated with periodic dates.

Always be on the lookout for ways to do things in organized and consistent ways. For example, store CSS styles only in specific files and places where you can manage them. When you are in a hurry to solve a formatting problem, it is easy to add a little CSS to fix the specific formatting issue. The problem comes later, when you want to make global changes to the styles. Thinking long-term is best.

> *Always be on the lookout for ways to do things in organized and consistent ways.*

CyberTips

As you set out to develop and maintain your website, there are many details to remember. Over the years as we have developed and maintained our church website, I have compiled a list of "CyberTips." Almost all these tips are the direct result of a not-so-nicely-learned

Almost all these tips are the direct result of a not-so-nicely-learned lesson.

lesson. My hope is that this list will help you experience fewer of these lessons! Although some tips are mentioned elsewhere in this book, they are repeated here for your reference. These are in no particular order.

1. The people on your team are more important than the task of building your website.
2. Start with static content first, and add changing content only as you are able to keep it up-to-date.
3. Don't post personal phone numbers or addresses without permission.
4. Never post private e-mail addresses; instead, create e-mail aliases.
5. Don't violate copyright laws, and especially watch out for copyrighted music.
6. Design for people with low-end PCs, modems, and 800-by-600 pixel monitors.
7. Keep the total page size with graphics under 150 kilobytes.
8. Use a common CSS file that can be cached by the browser.
9. Don't use frames.
10. Restrict page width to 760 pixels or less, or to 100 percent.
11. Don't use graphic backgrounds; white or black is usually best.
12. Don't make pages longer than three screens vertically.
13. Never require horizontal scrolling.
14. Keep the link colors the same throughout the website, and use an obvious color.
15. Never underline text, because it will look like a link.
16. Use animation sparingly and purposefully.
17. Never allow banner advertisements on a church website.
18. Include many pictures of people.
19. Get written permission to post pictures of kids; get at least verbal permission from adults.

20. Put a church logo or pictures of people on the front page instead of a picture of your church building.

21. Put the address of the church in the template footer.

22. Never put the words "under construction" or an "under construction" graphic anywhere on your website.

23. Provide an alternative to the back button in your navigation.

24. Use a CMS, and train many people to help maintain your website.

25. Let the people who generate the content enter the content.

26. Make sure pictures are resized to their final display size, not just resized with HTML.

27. Use JPGs for photos.

28. Use GIFs for animation and cartoons.

29. Consider design for viewing pages with PDAs and cell phones.

30. If at all possible, transcribe your sermons and post them in text format.

31. Minimize use of plug-ins and technology tricks.

32. Avoid Java applets.

33. Add interactive features and online community to your website.

34. Don't do this alone; get at least a few other people to help.

35. If someone posts something nasty to your website, make it a ministry opportunity.

36. Use fewer words; use words most people understand; remember that visitors may be from far away.

37. To make large blocks of text more readable, narrow the columns to less than 500 pixels wide.

38. Avoid mistakes, and make removing mistakes top priority.

39. Know from the start that this takes much longer than you would ever think.

40. Take security very, very, very seriously.

41. Remember that it is not about technology; it is about ministry.

42. Use standard XHTML.

43. Plan your folder structure, folder names, file naming, and styles.

44. Use Flash or video for communication, not just looks.

45. Don't use Flash for navigation.

46. Design for accessibility for the visually and hearing impaired.

47. Laugh at yourself when you mess up.

48. Don't use free online services that include ads.

49. Encrypt all posted e-mail addresses so spam spider programs can't get them. Answer e-mails promptly.

50. Don't use anything from another website without permission.

51. It is okay to link to other websites without asking.

52. Be very careful where you link, because people consider your links to be endorsements.

53. Just because you can legally use certain music in church does not mean you can legally post it on the web.

54. It is better to have missing information than wrong information on the website.

55. Provide an obvious way to contact the web team from the website to send suggestions and questions.

56. Limit use of PDF documents that need to be printed and complex documents that few people will read online.

57. Pray a lot for this ministry. Remember, this is a God thing!

58. Don't add a large set of links to other websites on a link page unless there are special reasons why your visitors need them.

59. Do not automatically start playing music or a video on a page unless a visitor clicks on a link just for this purpose.

60. Know that your website will go down; computers will fail; networks will fail.

61. Test your templates and unique pages with multiple browsers.

62. Link to a mapping website for a map to your church, but don't copy the map because that is a copyright violation.

63. Include the Global Positioning System (GPS) coordinates along with other church location information.

64. Never add a visitor counter to a webpage; you can find out how many visitors you have from the web server logs.

65. Consider a copyright notice on your pages. It is not required to protect them; it is just a reminder to visitors.

66. When in doubt, simple is usually better, especially for any actions visitors will need to take.

67. Break up text blocks with paragraph titles, bullet and numbered lists, graphics, and blank space.

68. If you have features that require a visitor to log on, try to limit each visitor to only one username and password.

69. Give visitors the option of playing media immediately via progressive download or downloading it to play later.

70. Avoid really large images or text blocks. Keep the relative sizes of text and graphics close to the same.

Helping Search Engines Find You

As explained in chapter 4, the three main ways to promote your website are: 1) promote it within and around your church; 2) register on websites that list churches; and 3) register your URL for search engines. There are a few other things you can do to your website that will help search engines incorporate your website contents into their search indexes.

Search engines, such as Google and Yahoo!, run special programs called "spiders," "crawlers," or "search bots" that browse websites, capture their pages, and index the words in the pages. This huge index is used to generate search results. The results are links to websites that match the visitor's search criteria. Spider programs run constantly. In order to avoid slowing down websites with many simultaneous requests, most spider programs request a few pages at a time and spread requests over time. Of course, they must return to your website again and again to see if any changes have been made. As you might guess, this is quite a mammoth task given the millions of websites on the internet. We can make it easier for these programs to "crawl" our websites, which in turn boosts our presence in the results lists.

Search engines run special programs called "spiders," "crawlers," or "search bots" that browse websites, capture their pages, and index the words in the pages.

Search engines rank results lists according to a measure of relevance. The goal is to have the most relevant and useful websites (based on the search criteria) listed first. High search-engine ranking can mean high profits, so search-engine companies keep private the details of the techniques they use to decide ranking, and they are constantly refining these techniques. Website developers work hard to get their websites ranked more highly. The process of trying to attain high search-engine ranking is called "Search Engine Optimization" (SEO). There are websites and books that teach SEO and even SEO businesses that claim to help companies increase their rankings. For churches, hiring someone is probably not affordable or necessary. Here are a few tips that will help you address the most critical SEO needs:

The most important thing you can do to increase your website's ranking is to focus on creating a great website with a lot of well-organized and useful content.

1. The most important thing you can do to increase your website's ranking is to focus on creating a great website with a lot of well-organized and useful content. Great websites naturally provide many good words that search engines will index.

2. Ensure that your website is standard XHTML so that search engines will understand and index the pages correctly.

3. Encourage other respectable websites to link to your

website. Search engines consider these links to be a "vote" for your website.

4. Think of the types of words visitors might use to look for your website, and include those words in the content of your webpages. Note that spider software cannot read words in graphics or in Flash, so it is best not to use graphics to display important words and titles.

5. Include an alternate-text and title tags that describe each graphic. Search engines index the content of these tags. Avoid hidden text and links because search engines may consider them deceptive. Include descriptive page title and header tags.

6. Avoid using a CMS that cannot create standard looking URLs. Standard URLs are made up of a domain, some number of directories separated by slashes, an optional filename, and optional parameters—for example, http://Domain.org/aboutus/staff. Most CMS systems generate all pages using one main script file. From a search engine's perspective, all the pages on the website appear to be one page with parameters sent to it—for example, http://Domain.org/index.php?id=2 ("2" identifies the page). The TYPO3 CMS supports standard URLS, so it works fine with search engines.

7. Add some basic meta tags to your pages. Meta tags provide additional information about your website and its contents, but do not display on a webpage in a browser. Meta tags are placed between the start and end of the head tag (between <head> and </head>). They are usually formatted like this: <meta name="NameAttribute" content="the content of the meta tag">, where NameAttribute is a predefined name or one that you created. The most valuable predefined meta tag name attributes are probably "description" and "keywords." Using "description," you provide a short description of the website or page. Using "keywords," you provide a list of keywords for the page. Here is an example: <meta name="keywords" content="Christian, Church, Jesus">. Feel free to use many keywords. Use each word only one time, and include both singular and plural versions if visitors might enter either as

a search word. TYPO3 provides support for automated meta tag generation.

Website Statistics

Once your website is up and running, the obvious questions is, "How many people are coming to the website, and which pages are they viewing?" Most web servers have log files where every "hit" (web-server transaction) is recorded. Information logged includes: 1) the type of request, 2) the file/page requested, 3) parameters that were exchanged, 4) the previous page the visitor was browsing, and 5) the date and time. The log also includes visitor information such as: 1) browser type, 2) IP address, 3) computer type, 4) operating system, and 5) other computer settings. There is a wealth of information in the log, but the concept of hits is not very meaningful. A visitor browsing a webpage will generate any number of hits depending on the files needed to display the page, including all graphics files. Browser cache adds to the confusion because sometimes a browser will use a cached version of a file, and that will not generate a hit. So the logs contain many details, but the log file information in its raw form is not very valuable.

Most web servers have log files where every "hit" (web-server transaction) is recorded.

Web servers usually come with web-log analysis ("stats") software that processes the log files. TYPO3 supports creation and analysis of logs using a popular open source program called AWStats. A stats program summarizes the log files and provides some extremely useful information. For example, the stats show how many times a specific page was requested. We really don't know if a visitor stopped to read the page or not; we only know that the web server received the request and sent out the page. This information is still helpful because it tells us which pages on the website are most popular. The stats program will usually help by listing the pages in order of popularity. Stats use the logged computer IP address and lookups on the internet to figure out visitors' internet service providers and even the countries they are visiting from. This is how we know that people from over fifty different

A stats program summarizes the log files and provides some extremely useful information.

countries visit the Ginghamsburg website each month. We can also find out the percentage of our visitors that use each type of browser. So the stats provide quite a bit of visitor information.

You might have noticed that we do not know how many different people visit a website. It is not possible to deduce that. The second best thing is to count visits. A visit is an occasion when a person who comes to the website browses one or more pages and then leaves. If they leave and come back fifteen minutes or more later, then that is counted as another visit. Using a combination of information in the logs, the stats program can estimate visits fairly accurately. Visits from search engine spiders are ignored in the process. Most web administrators use visits as the primary measure of traffic to their websites. When I am backed into a corner and must provide a guess at the number of different human visitors coming to the website, I usually estimate by dividing the number of monthly visits by ten.

I encourage you to experiment with your stats software. You can look at the information in so many different ways, and it is fun to play with. At Ginghamsburg, I report this information to our staff leadership and to the CyberMinistry team each month. It helps us all get a better understanding of the impact of our ministry. Over the years it has been exciting to see our visits increase from ten to one hundred to over one thousand per day. It is great to have a tool that can help us monitor progress, and it is a real blessing to know that people are benefiting from our efforts. We are blessed to serve.

Keeping It Going and Growing

Creating an excellent internet ministry is more about perseverance than brilliance. It is important to think of your internet ministry as an ongoing long-term ministry and not as a project to create a website. Projects can be complete; ministries are never complete. If you stick with it, your internet ministry can grow over time to enhance the other ministries in your church as they each add a web component. The internet is not going to decline; it will only get bigger and more pervasive throughout all aspects of our lives and the life of the church.

Creating an excellent internet ministry is more about perseverance than brilliance.

CHAPTER 9

WE LEARNED THAT CONNECTING PEOPLE MAKES MINISTRY HAPPEN

Creating healthy online communities

What an amazing woman! She is more connected to both God and people than anyone else I know. I am in awe of her passion for living and her confidence that God is in control. She has the kind of faith and wisdom I long for.

Pat was an amazing person. When I told her that, she was somewhat embarrassed and told me I would never want to be like her because she had such evil thoughts. I had to laugh as I imagined the kind of evil thoughts a godly older woman might have. She was a humble servant who was well aware of her sin and totally devoted to the Lord. I listened carefully to anything she said, and I watched how she conducted her life.

Pat loved to write, and she was the right person to form and lead the CyberMinistry Reflection Team—a group of passionate and gifted writers, all unpaid servants, who create daily reflections (devotionals) for our website. Since everyone on the Reflection Team worked from home on their own computers, we set up an online forum to enable them to keep in touch. At the time, internet ministry was new; and it was common for people to warn me how cold and impersonal internet technology was because it did not connect people in personal relationships. I was curious to see how this team would work, given that we were using this "cold and impersonal" technology to stay in touch. I had a feeling it would work okay.

Pat took charge in her humble yet confident way. She posted to the forum frequently and got the team going quickly. The posts included assignments and lots of encouraging words. Pat clearly had the gift of encouragement. She called the team the "God Pencils," and reminded them that their task as writers was to write down what God was telling them. The team responded with posts that kept a flow of online discussion going. As time went on, I noticed that the online discussions were not the only business of the team. People would share personal needs and prayer requests. For the first time, I saw full prayers posted to a forum. The prayers even ended in "Amen." The group became a close community even though many of them had not met face-to-face. In her quiet but firm way, Pat was like the mom of this online family. She was the strong one who loved everyone, instructed them, and even scolded them at times. This was, and still is today, a very healthy and supportive online community.

When we learned that Pat had lung cancer, roles began to change. Pat shared her difficulties and occasional victories, and the group became the "strong one" who supported and prayed for Pat. Her immune system became so weak that no one could visit her in person, and the telephone was just too intrusive. Posting to the forum was our only method of communication, so we used it to learn how she was doing and to support her.

Throughout this, her strong faith and sense of humor continued to amaze me. She asked for prayer for healing from the sickness and weakness caused by the cancer treatments. She talked about the silver-haired wig she bought to hide her hair loss. When she was at a store wearing her wig, someone complimented her on how beautiful her hair was. She said that she told them, "Thank you." She told us that it was not a lie—that it was, in fact, her hair since she paid for it herself. I laughed until I cried, then prayed for her.

Even when she knew she was very ill, she continued to schedule writing and to lead and encourage the team. Sometimes I would briefly forget she was sick. A few months before her death, she wrote, "Hi, all you God-fearing Pencils, you! …Even though time is marching by fast, I just want to take a minute to thank all of you so very much for your faithfulness to this ministry. You are all so very, very better, better, best! What a privilege to be your teammate…As always, looking forward with joyful anticipation as to what your God-messages will be this time. And if the Spirit moves you to send your devotions in early, I will praise His Holy Name and you, too. Take care and may God bless you indeed!"

As her body weakened, and she shared her struggles and requested prayer, the posted prayers continued at an increasing rate. "Dear Father in Heaven, we lift our sister Pat into your loving and healing arms..." "Father, I lift up Pat to you. I ask for mercies for these two warriors of yours..." "Thank you Father, that you have called us to cast every care upon you, because you care. We give our precious Pat to you..." "Dear Heavenly Father, we thank you for the warrior you have graced us with in Pat..." Pat was showered with prayer and love from the team.

After Pat passed away in November 2002, the team grieved, comforted, and rejoiced together via the online forum. Many writers on the team shared personal stories of how Pat had changed their lives and taught them. I learned I was one of many who looked to her as a model of Christian faith. Her family told me that in her last days, when she could barely get out of bed, she would muster up enough energy to go to her computer to read the posts from the team, but she was too weak to respond. The family said they also printed them and read them to her. She received the prayers and love even when we thought she was not getting them.

Needless to say, we learned a lot from Pat; and I was blessed to know that we were a comfort to her as well. And it all happened in online community. In fact, we could not have made these close, personal connections if not for internet technology—the technology some people think of as cold. Since that time, we have seen over and over that internet technology can be a powerful tool to connect with and minister to people. In many cases, the online community ministers more than the web content we work so hard to produce. In honor of Pat, here is one of the team's favorite devotionals she wrote.

My Get Up and Go, Got Up and Went...

"Oh, Lord, is that the alarm clock going off at this ungodly hour? It can't be. Seems like I just got to bed! What time is it, anyway?"

"Good morning, Pat. It's time to get up and go. Is there a problem?"

"Who said that?"

"I did. The Lord. You did ask me a question didn't you? Or were you using my name loosely again? I have been meaning to talk to you about that!"

"I'm sorry, Lord. No, I really didn't mean to use your name in vain. It's just that I'm so tired. It seems like my get up and go, got up and went. There are so many things to do, Lord. So many different paths I must go down, or up. Not always sure which way to go. So many people and things need so much of my time. Incidentally, those vitamins the pharmacist gave me haven't helped a bit. So, what say you, Lord? Where do I go?"

"Well, Pat, what you're doing right now is a step in the right direction. You're asking me for a solution instead of trying to figure it out for yourself, as you usually do. That's another thing I've been meaning to talk to you about when you can spare me a minute or two! You are in a spiritual funk right now. But remember, my child, no one else has put you there. You did it yourself. So if you're ready to listen, I am more than ready, willing, and able to help."

"Thank you, Lord. I'm ready to listen. I really want to be on a successful Jesus journey. I enjoy the things you set before me and let me..."

"Pat! You're doing it again!"

"What, Lord? What am I doing?"

"For one thing, you're not listening! Now settle down. O.K.? O.K.! I know you want to walk the same path as my Son did, but you must remember to keep focused on His star. Don't expend your energies in so many directions that you become so weary you can't see your way clear to reach the goal you are seeking. Remember, Pat, your first goal should be to experience me. To diligently search for me in my Word. And then to listen to what I will tell you. That's the real journey I want you to be on."

"The world is waiting for you to tell them what I have made known to you. But you have to keep focused on me. Don't you know I have a perfect plan for your life force? Trust me to show you the way. Stop getting bogged down in a lifestyle of expending your energies on unproductive and unimportant self-styled goals. They'll just make you tired, my child. And I want you wired! Wired into my life force. Into my Spirit. Now, then, you asked me what time it was. What time do you think it is?"

"Well, Lord, from what you said, evidently now is the time to tell the world what you have made known to me. So I've decided it's time to keep focused on you and let my get up and go, get up and go. To commit to the real journey of knowing you and your love and know that there is nothing that can happen to me that you and I together can't handle!"

What's Online Community?

Online community happens when online visitors connect in discussion and relationship. Online community is different from most other website features because the visitors provide the content. The web team provides the rules of the community, the topics, and the mechanism to connect. There are many different web tools that can create opportunities for online community: chat, instant messenger, e-mail lists, forums, blogs, connectors, wikis, polls, comments, and ratings. Like most tools, each of these has pros and cons in different ministry situations. This chapter will help you understand the features of each of these tools, where the tools fit in ministry, and challenges you may face as you use them.

Online community happens when online visitors connect in discussion and relationship.

Allowing visitors to type in whatever they would like to type and then post it onto a page on your website can be scary. There are fears of what people might post, of the malicious people this option might attract, and of the online conversation getting out of control. We have included forums on our website since 1997, and we have added many other community features as well. Since then, we have had a few minor incidents, but they are miniscule compared to the incredible ministry we have seen. Adding community features is not without risk. By its nature, ministry that connects with people can get dirty and risky now and then. However, take precautions to minimize the risks, and the ministry benefit will far outweigh the difficulties. I encourage you to incorporate some form of online community into your internet ministry. The ministry opportunities are worth it.

Chat and Instant Messenger

Chat is one of the older forms of online community and Instant Messenger (IM) is one of the newer ones. With chat, visitors connect to an online address referred to as a "chat room," where they "type to talk" to others. As visitors type and submit their messages, everyone currently connected to the chat room immediately sees each new message. Each message is labeled with the username of the visitor who posted it and with the time of the post. A busy chat room can produce a constant flow of messages as each new message is added to the bottom of the list. Chat users need to know the chat server address and the name of the chat room to join in the community, but they do not need to know each other's usernames. For this reason, chat rooms can become great meeting places.

The challenge with using chat on a church website is that it must be moderated at all times because problems can occur rapidly and without warning. It is usually best to turn chat rooms on only at specific times and then to turn them off when they are no longer monitored. Moderating may include intervening in the discussion, blocking specific users, or stopping the chat. Chat can be fun and works well for all kinds of live online discussion. For example, you could try a live chat with your pastor or with a visiting Christian music artist before a concert in your area. In order to avoid the hassle of requiring special software on each visitor's computer host chat on your own church website. Look for software that uses AJAX technology. AJAX (Asynchronous JavaScript and XML) allows a web browser to maintain a live connection to the web server, and a live connection enables the chat discussion to dynamically update within the visitors' browsers. This makes it easy for visitors to connect to your live chat room using nothing more than a standard browser. Also, since chat conversations go by so quickly, use chat software that is capable of logging the entire discussion, so that you can go back and review it.

IM is similar to chat because IM users also type to talk. IM is unlike chat because connections are directly between people who know each other's IM names, and although more can be added, IM connections are usually between two people. With IM no connection can take place unless at least one participant knows the username of another participant and initiates a connection. Chat is like a physical room where people can gather in an ad hoc way to discuss a topic, but IM is more like a phone call or a conference call where the participants are specified ahead of time. IM is a very popular form of communication. IM fits well at times when a phone call would be a little too intrusive. It works great for ministry teams that need to stay in touch, and youth leaders will find it a popular way to communicate with youth. We use it a lot to communicate among our CyberMinistry team. When you have a quick question or want to pass along some information, it is amazing how handy it is to send a quick message via IM.

IM depends on special servers on the internet that know your username, can tell others your online status, and can enable the IM connection. There are several companies that provide IM servers including America Online (AOL), Microsoft Network (MSN) and Yahoo!. Due to the popularity of these services and the need for people to connect through these common servers, it does not usually make sense to host IM on your church web server. This is one case where using a free commercial service is best. Using IM requires special software running on each visitor's computer, and a free individual account on one of the IM services. Without additional (free) software, it is only possible to connect to one service at a time using that service's software, so I recommend getting IM software that can support multiple services, such as Trillian.

Both chat and IM establish community with live text-based communications. The advantage they have over e-mail is that the exchange of messages is immediate and seems more like normal conversation. From a ministry perspective, one issue with chat is that visitors may feel alienated if they type poorly or have a difficult time with writing and spelling. In general this is not an issue since the online culture is usually not too concerned about grammar and spelling. In fact, schoolteachers cringe at the sight of most online messaging. Another issue is that, unlike e-mail or forums, visitors need to communicate at the same point in time. Synchronizing schedules can be difficult, especially if you want to meet online with several people at the same time.

Both chat and IM establish community with live text-based communications.

E-mail Lists

The first thing most people learn when they get internet access is how to use e-mail, so e-mail is a useful tool for ministry because we can assume that the majority of people will know how to use it. E-mail, as you can infer from its name, is the electronic version of paper mail. E-mail lists use standard e-mail, but instead of sending one message to one person, the lists distribute a single e-mail to many different e-mail addresses. Software called an "e-mail list server," or a "listserv," performs this task. This software receives a single e-mail sent to a special list-server e-mail address and then replicates and sends that e-mail to all the e-mail addresses included on a subscriber list. The one key feature of mailing lists that differentiates them from other community tools is that e-mails are "pushed" out to the subscribers. In other words, the messages come to each subscriber automatically—subscribers don't have to go to a website to get the information. If you need to get a message to a large group of people as quickly as possible, then an e-mail list is a good solution.

E-mail is a useful tool for ministry because we can assume that the majority of people will know how to use it.

Please note that if you set up an e-mail list that supports sending e-mail attachments, it is vital that you also have virus protection on the server to ensure the list does not send out a virus to every subscriber. I have seen this happen, and it does not result in a good feeling! For this reason, and also because attachments can fill visitor e-mail boxes, consider turning off attachments for public e-mail lists.

There are two common configurations for e-mail lists. First, there are lists where a limited number of people are allowed to send e-mail to a group of subscribers. These are ideal for church newsletters and announcements. You can also use them for a daily devotional or to send information to a particular group, like all the small group leaders. This type of list works best when a few people need to get information to a group of people and when you prefer that members of the group be unable to send e-mail to the entire group. The second type of list is one in which any subscriber can send e-mail to all the other subscribers. These can work well to support topical discussions, small groups, and ministry teams. They work best for groups that do not have a lot of discussion and where the discussion does not need to be stored and viewed later.

We once had about fifteen or twenty different mailing lists. Some of them grew to several hundred subscribers; as the community grew, the frequency of e-mails kept increasing. This was exciting because there was so much interaction. It felt like a really healthy online community. Then, to our surprise, people started unsubscribing in droves. At first we did not know why. Then we learned that when the number of e-mails reached ten to twenty per day, subscribers felt they were getting too much e-mail, so they unsubscribed. They loved the mailing lists, but could not keep up with all the posts. We offered a digest option that put all e-mails for one day into one e-mail, but that did not help—it was still too much to read. It was surprising to find that the success of a group ended up driving people away from the group. We tried splitting the group into multiple groups with slightly different topics, but that did not seem to help either. Adding to the difficulty were increasing numbers of new subscribers who often posted questions that previous new subscribers had already asked. The brand-new subscribers had no way of knowing this since they could not see previous posts. We simply had too many posts, and some posts were repeats. More visitors unsubscribed, and the CyberTeam became less popular because of the frustration we created. We learned that we needed a different approach. We ended up moving all our e-mail list groups to a different community tool called forums. E-mail lists typically work well for smaller groups; we inadvertently used them in a way that did not work well because of the number of e-mails.

Forums

Forums, which are also called "bulletin boards" or "discussion groups," enable visitors to participate in online community on your website. Visitors post messages and read messages that other visitors have posted. Forums links are usually gathered on a main page that lists several forum names and additional information about each forum. Visitors can choose a forum and then read current messages, post new messages, or reply to existing messages. The flow of the conversation from an initial posted message to replies to more replies is often called a "thread."

Forums store all the messages in a database, which is an advantage over e-mail lists because visitors can view previous messages. This helps avoid the e-mail list problem of repeat messages from brand-new subscribers. Storing the messages can also make a forum into an online reference tool. Using the forum search capability, visitors can locate and read though discussions that took place in the past.

Forums store all the messages in a database, which is an advantage over e-mail lists because visitors can view previous messages.

Our CyberMinistry team uses a private forum to store information on how to do specific website technical tasks and to announce when we have made software changes. This is how we document what we have learned and what we have done. We can also discuss it online. If there is a need, we can always find the messages later.

Forum software features vary. For example, forums can include message-popularity ratings based on visitor votes, ability to attach a file to a message, ability to display a personal graphic next to each visitor's messages, and ability to send newly posted messages via e-mail. The ability to send e-mails containing newly posted messages provides some of the benefits of an e-mail list. The main difference between forums with automatic e-mail and e-mail lists is the way visitors post messages. With forums, visitors post messages using a web form on the forum. With e-mail lists, visitors post messages by sending an e-mail to a special e-mail address. Forums give each individual the option of receiving messages via e-mail or via a web browser. With forums, a visitor can stop receiving messages via e-mail by simply changing a user setting. Unlike e-mail lists, forums have the benefit of archiving previous messages. For most of our online groups, both public and private, we now use a forum that has e-mail capability. Visitors may find forums harder to use than e-mail; however, archival and optional e-mail make forums an excellent tool for online community.

Blogs

A blog, which is short for "web log," is a community tool that enables one person or sometimes a small group of people to post a series of messages over time. The blog messages are listed in reverse chronological order with the most recent message at the top of the page. The people posting the messages are called "bloggers," and they are the "owners" of the blog. Blogs are not usually grouped by subject like forums. So if a website has multiple independent bloggers, then there will be a separate blog page for each blogger. Visitors can comment on specific posted messages, but the focus of a blog is on the blogger's messages. In fact, reading the visitors' comments usually requires going to a separate comment page. Like forum entries, blog entries remain stored in a database. Blogs usually have options for finding previous blog messages by date, topic, or keyword search.

A blog is a community tool that enables one person or sometimes a small group of people to post a series of messages over time.

Since blogs are usually owned by one person, the messages tend to be informally written and topics are whatever the blogger wants to write about. Some bloggers use blogs as a personal diary. Others tend to blog about one main topic. Some share news. In general, visitors expect bloggers to post frequently. Many bloggers post daily; some post a few times a week. Within a church, blogs are useful for informal communications from a church leader like a pastor or a youth director. The informal nature of blogs makes them feel more personal and friendly, which makes them a good way to communicate in a church. Plus, they can be fun and are easy to use. If you minister to people who have blogs, then it may be helpful to read their blogs to prepare you to serve them better.

Connectors

"Connector" is a term I use to define a different type of community that we created in the Web-Empowered Church. A connector community is designed to help people who have a need connect with people who can address that need, and to help people who can offer a service connect with people who can use that service. Anyone can publicly post a message containing a need (like a prayer request) or service (like a job opening); however, a reply to a connector message does not get posted publicly. The reply is automatically e-mailed back to the originator, so only the originator of the

A connector community is designed to help people who have a need connect with people who can address that need, and to help people who can offer a service connect with people who can use that service.

message receives the reply message. If the need is fulfilled or the service is used up, then the originator removes the posted message. Connector messages are not archived because they are no longer needed once they are fulfilled. The Web-Empowered Church connector can be set to automatically remove messages that are older than a specified number of days.

Wikis

A wiki is a webpage that any visitor or specific group of visitors can edit. This may sound unusual, but with a wiki, visitors can add content to the page, and they can also modify or delete existing content. A wiki is like a big, public whiteboard to which anyone can add in any way and from which anyone can erase anything. Visitors use a somewhat unique language to edit the wiki page; however, the language is not difficult to figure out, especially when modifying existing pages. The most famous wiki-based website is probably Wikipedia.org, an online encyclopedia. Wikis work well for collaborative activities such as brainstorming, creating a list, or

A wiki is a webpage that any visitor or a specific group of visitors can edit.

writing a document. They can also be interesting on a youth website. In my personal experience, some visitors are intimidated by having complete ability to modify the page and may not post anything at all. If you try using a wiki, encourage everyone to feel free to participate.

Polls

A poll is a multiple-choice question that visitors answer. Most polls are automatically tallied so visitors can see a summary of results as soon as they respond. Polls add interactivity and interest to a website. Polls help build community as visitors get a sense of the way the entire community is responding. We include a poll question on the front page of the Ginghamsburg website each week. This question is designed to get people thinking about the topic of the coming week's sermon.

You can also use polls to gather practical information about visitors. We created a poll question that asked visitors to tell us the speed of their internet connections. You could ask them about Bible version preference or frequency of church attendance. Please note that if polls are used for an important purpose, it is difficult to guarantee that visitors do not vote more than once. While polls can be fun, I recommend that you do not count on their accuracy too heavily.

Comments and Ratings

Comments are opportunities for visitors to type remarks about anything on the current page. Ratings are a way that visitors assign value to the content on a page. These two mechanisms provide interactivity and community. For example, a youth website might have a set of pages featuring Christian music artists. Adding comments or a rating system to these pages makes them more popular, interesting, and fun.

Getting Community Started

Online community happens in an environment that provides healthy social interaction, exchange of opinions, requests and responses, and useful information. Creating and maintaining such an environment requires a deliberate effort. One of the most challenging aspects of establishing an online community is keeping it fresh and active. Setting up many different groups is easy, but getting an active discussion going in each group can be a challenge. We've found that a group needs multiple participants posting multiple messages to grow, so we start with fewer groups to allow visitors to focus on only those groups.

Once a small set of groups has been created, discussion in each group needs to begin. Most people are reluctant to post messages to a community without messages or with just a few messages. Here is one technique that may help get the ball rolling. Gather a small team of people who are interested in supporting a group. Ask the team to begin a discussion and rekindle it as necessary. Ask the team to use the community to discuss topics of common interest to most visitors of that group. The purpose is to get the momentum

Most people are reluctant to post messages to a community without messages or with just a few messages.

going, build up the number of posted messages, and hopefully have a beneficial conversation in the process. Visitors will see the good discussion and join in. Even if they don't join in, many visitors will "listen in" on the discussion and benefit from it without actually posting messages. These visitors are referred to as "lurkers." It is not uncommon for visitors who are active in the group to claim to have been lurkers for over a year.

Keeping Healthy

Moderators are responsible for helping maintain a healthy online environment by monitoring every message.

We have found that every online group develops a culture of its own. It is amazing how two groups that are next to each other on the screen will have such different visitors who participate in them. To maintain a healthy culture, assign moderators to each group. ("Group" here means every individual community, no matter what specific community tool is used.) Moderators are responsible for helping maintain a healthy online environment by monitoring every message and ensuring that the messages do not violate the community's rules, which should be posted on the website. Our rules are simple:

1. Please keep your messages short and on topic.
2. Please respect others.
3. No solicitations please.

To maintain a healthy online culture, the moderator needs to act at the first sign of messages that are rude, crude, or advertising. Moderators can post responses that help defuse problems before they grow. Moderators can also remove inappropriate messages, but we have found that this can upset the posters. Instead of removing such posts, we edit them to make them less offensive. This approach has the benefit of showing the poster how to write more appropriately and respectfully while allowing the message to remain online. For more serious cases, moderators can contact the individual directly via e-mail and respectfully explain the issue. If treated respectfully, most people will discontinue posting inappropriate messages. In fact, many people will apologize to the group once they realize they have posted inappropriately.

Moderators may occasionally need to send e-mail to visitors who post too often, post off topic, or otherwise disrupt the group. A disruption is identified by comments in visitor messages or complaint e-mails sent to the moderator. It is best to explain the situation and ask the offenders to post less frequently and more appropriately, thereby giving everyone an opportunity to participate. Most frequent posters do not realize their behavior is offensive, and they adjust their posting accordingly. The moderator is not trying to control the group but to keep the group healthy and safe.

Moderators are also responsible for making sure requests receive responses in a reasonable amount of time, even if they need to do the research themselves. It is frustrating to post a question and not receive a response. We used to assign different monitors to each group, but keeping enough moderators assigned and trained became difficult. Now we use team moderation. Three team members receive all messages from every type of community on the entire website. We hope that at least one member of the team will be available to take action if something needs immediate attention. And that action is often not the task of asking someone to post more appropriately. More frequently, we are alerted of an urgent need, and we need to get help for someone. A moderator who is an active participant in the group will know the visitors in the community better, but our team moderation approach has worked fine too. As you would expect, the moderator team can get a lot of e-mails. However, we do not read each message in great detail. Instead, we skim for inflammatory words and solicitations. The review of each message usually goes very fast.

It is frustrating to post a question and not receive a response.

Difficult Visitors

Membership in online communities is varied, and groups sometimes include difficult visitors. Consider a difficult visitor as a ministry opportunity. It is not logical for someone to come to a church website and be rude to others unless there is some issue with which he or she is struggling. This behavior is probably a cry for help, or at least an indication that the person is hurting. As is often said, hurting people hurt people. We want to help them if we can. At the same time, this type of visitor can damage a healthy online community, and other visitors may choose to leave the community. We need ways to maintain the healthy community while we help the

Consider a difficult visitor as a ministry opportunity. difficult visitor individually. Our experience has been that, with over three thousand registered users, only two or three difficult people per year disrupt online community.

In online community that is freely available to the public, it is difficult to totally stop determined and malicious visitors from posting inappropriate messages. Some communities can filter specific words, usually profanity. If you have this option, enable it and consider adding some additional words to the filter list. Another option is to remove a difficult visitor's account. In our experience, this approach causes the visitor to become increasingly angry and does not send the right message when it comes from a church. Churches should not reject anyone, because God does not reject anyone. And, technically capable visitors can be back online with a new account in very little time. It is seldom wise to delete or modify accounts. Another solution is to change the community setting to moderated, which stops automatic posting of messages. New messages are held from public view until a specified moderator approves them. We try hard to avoid doing this because it reduces the immediacy of the community. Turning on moderation and manually rejecting messages from malicious visitors may tire the visitors so they will quit trying. Of course, this is only for the most difficult cases, which will probably be rare.

The options for connecting with difficult visitors are posting messages to the entire group or directly e-mailing the difficult visitors. Publicly posting can embarrass them and ordinarily does not help them or the group. Instead, it is usually best to begin with respectful e-mail exchanges, of which the goal is to develop a relationship, understand the purpose of the messages, and ask for their help in respecting the rules of the group. It is also best to encourage direct e-mail exchanges instead of posts to the entire group, which can cause additional disruption. For more difficult challenges, getting people connected with trained people who can help them is important. I call on people from our counseling center when the emotional need seems significant. Then, a counselor works with the difficult visitor via e-mail or phone. Through this method, we have been able to help people through some rough times. I have personally exchanged e-mails with, and prayed for, difficult visitors for months after an incident. They matter to us and to God.

I strongly suggest that you do not let visitors post on your website without registering for an account that has a verified e-mail address associated with it. If they do not provide a valid e-mail address, then there is no way to contact them directly; and the only option for communication becomes the public community. Verify the e-mail address by having the registration software send an e-mail containing a randomly generated unique link back to the website. When the visitor receives the e-mail and clicks on the link, the e-mail address is automatically verified and the new account is enabled. This approach ensures that each e-mail address is valid. To reverify e-mail addresses, send an e-mail to everyone with an account, then remove accounts for e-mail addresses that are rejected (bounce). We try to verify e-mail addresses yearly.

Do not let visitors post on your website without registering for an account that has a verified e-mail address associated with it.

One of our biggest challenges has been avoiding messages that are focused more on selling something than on the group topic or community. These are a form of spam—undesired and intrusive advertising—but they are not always blatant spam, and can be disruptive to a group. An example is a web developer who constantly refers to her ability to help (for a fee) visitors in the group. It seems as though the purpose of her involvement is solely to divert the discussion and attract new attention to her business. Some people are less subtle and post typical spam messages. As spammers have told us, the attraction to spammers is that a given group provides easy access to a targeted audience of potential customers—new business is just one post away. For example, we have a motorcycle ministry that has its own forum. If a visitor has a business that customizes motorcycles, then he or she may be tempted to advertise on the forum. We don't mind occasional discussion about a business or product, but we do mind when messages feel like commercials.

We usually use the same techniques with spammers that we use with other difficult visitors. We e-mail them directly and ask them not to post advertisements. In a few cases this has not worked. As a last resort to address the problem, we post a message to the entire group. We inform the group of our efforts to stop the spammer's messages via repeated private e-mail exchanges. We tell the group that the spammer has continued to defy the group rules. We then ask the group to collectively agree to boycott the spammer's product or service. Members of the group are usually quick to post messages supporting the boycott. So far, this technique has worked well, and the spammers have immediately discontinued posting messages.

How Community Works

We have learned a lot about how communities work as we have experienced hosting online community over the years at Ginghamsburg Church. This may sound obvious, but one thing we have learned is that online community is a whole lot like face-to-face community. Visitors are people communicating via a different mechanism, but they are still people. What follows are a few of the issues we have noticed over the years. We have not conducted scientific, psychological analysis; these are merely observations and experiences that might be helpful to you.

Intimidation: We have been surprised at how many visitors are reluctant to post a message to a group. Some say they are unsure about the technology or don't want to show their ignorance. Others seem to be concerned that the group will respond negatively to a posted message. In the beginning most people are intimidated by the technology, and this keeps them from posting messages even when they would like to. The result is many lurkers. We estimate that about 90 percent of visitors are lurkers—those who read but do not post messages. At the same time, we've found that once visitors begin posting messages, much of their fear goes away, and we generally see more messages from them in the future.

Anonymity: By its nature, posting messages to a community is more anonymous than many other types of conversation. As a result, once visitors overcome the intimidation of the technology and of posting a message, they are likely to share personal stories. The anonymous feeling of online community allows visitors to express themselves more freely. Online community can also break down human barriers for those who are of different cultures or races, shy or uncomfortable around people, or self-conscious about their appearance. From a ministry perspective, the anonymity may allow us to have more open and frank discussions and to help people with various life issues. We also need to keep an eye out for visitors who are not who they claim to be. This problem is partially alleviated by the requirement to register with a valid e-mail address. Visitors know that we can contact them if needed. So far, the challenge of visitors pretending to be someone they are not has not been a problem for us.

> *Online community can also break down human barriers for those who are of different cultures or races, shy or uncomfortable around people, or self-conscious about their appearance.*

Group Environment: We have learned that each group takes on a unique environment defined by the visitors who post most of the messages. Groups vary on the formality of the discussion, acceptance of differing opinions and debate, acceptance of new visitors ("newbies"), desire to help others, and sense of community. Visitors will not stay in the group if they don't like the environment. Some of our groups have gotten into strong debates that lead to angry messages and personal attacks. This can quickly impact the health of the group, so it is important for the moderator to address these issues quickly and make sure the situation is resolved.

> *Each group takes on a unique environment defined by the visitors who post most of the messages.*

Peer Pressure: We did not anticipate the significance of peer pressure. Peer pressure is often what keeps the group healthy. We consider a group healthy if the group can police itself. One example of this behavior is when someone makes a rude comment, and one or two others post messages that let the originator of the comment know their behavior is unacceptable. Comments like, "Hey, no need to get nasty," or "Please cut the person some slack," are signs of peer pressure in action. We find that occasional peer pressure is a useful tool to help guide the group. Because peer pressure keeps people accountable, there are probably fewer problems with online community than most churches anticipate.

Relationships: We have seen online community facilitate close relationships. We have groups where most visitors have never met each other, yet many members consider the group to be their close friends. They know about each other's family and jobs, and talk about all sorts of issues. We had one group decide to get together for a live pizza party. It was fascinating to see how close people could be who had not met face-to-face. The group was like a family and had a great time together. They still continue the relationship online.

Team Collaboration: One power of online community is facilitating team collaboration. We have multiple teams that only occasionally meet in person, yet they are in frequent conversation online via collaborative community. We use private forums to make announcements, task team members, discuss plans, request assistance, get to know people, and more. The forums allow team members to participate when time permits and from any location. The forum also keeps all team members in the loop so everyone knows what is happening within the team. The result is team members who are informed and feel like they are part of the team without the need for frequent meetings. This is especially true of our Reflection and CyberMinistry teams.

Technical Support: Web ministries commonly get requests for assistance with activities such as registering for an account, resetting a password, subscribing to receive messages via e-mail, changing an e-mail address, and removing an account. Visitors can do all these things via available pages, but many of them find it too difficult or are unwilling to learn. We used to e-mail instructions on how to perform the functions, but this confused them more, and often resulted in more e-mail exchanges and increased frustration for all. Now, we make the changes and return an e-mail to say that the requested change was made. Visitors appear to be satisfied with this approach, and we have found that the technical support team spends less time making the changes than they used to spend describing how to make the changes.

A Good Thing

Community-based web tools are valuable additions to a church website and a major component of future internet ministry. Even though the effort to initiate and maintain online community can be significant, the ministry benefits can be much greater. We have received numerous e-mails from visitors all over the world who thanked us for our community features. We also find that teams can develop more synergy when they use online community to stay in touch. Community-based web tools connect people to people and allow them to work and learn together. Visitors can participate whenever they have time and from wherever they are located. Online community works especially well for congregations because a church is by definition a community.

Community-based web tools are valuable additions to a church website and a major component of future internet ministry.

CHAPTER 10

INNOVATIVE IDEAS THAT MAY WORK FOR YOUR CHURCH

Various examples of applying internet technology to web-empower church ministries

It's a web-empowered church!

Asixteen-year-old student goes to his computer to check out the youth leader's blog, where he learns there is a mission trip coming up. He sees that the youth leader is online, so he contacts the youth leader via instant messenger to ask about the mission trip. The youth leader tells him more about the trip and sends him a link to a webpage containing all the trip details. He suggests that the student check out the photo slide show and the daily log from last year's trip. The youth leader asks how the student has been doing and says he looks forward to seeing the student at youth group this week. The student gets on the online youth forums and posts a question asking if anyone else is going on the trip because it sounds really cool. He then sends his parents an e-mail with a link to a page that provides all the details about the trip, the costs, and a form that allows them to sign up and pay for the trip online.

A single parent wakes up before her children do, and the chaos of the day starts. She goes online to do her daily devotion and journaling. She is really touched by the day's Scripture reading, so she writes in her private online journal and then decides to post her thoughts to the public discussion group where she can share with others who are following along in the same devotional. She attends church each week and likes to pray for others, so she chooses to receive all church prayer requests via e-mail using the online prayer system. She carefully reads through the requests and prays for each of them. Next, she goes to the single-parent forum and reads through the latest posts from other Christian single parents. Online they talk about the challenges of single parenting, pray for each other, and plan events that they do together as a group. When times are difficult, the single-parent forum helps her keep it all together. She has friends there whom she can get to quickly and who understand the challenges of single parenting.

A businessperson travels and works a lot of hours, including frequent trips on the weekends. There are few chances for him to participate at church events, but he does so whenever he can. While traveling he uses his laptop to connect to the church website, where he watches the sermons every week via progressive downloaded video. He is also taking an online class at the church. The teaching is available via video, and he can download the written class resources and assignments. The class includes an online discussion area, where he posts questions to which the teacher and others taking the class respond. He is also in a private online men's accountability group where a handful of brothers in Christ share openly and keep each other accountable. They get together in person whenever they can, but their busy schedules make an online group a good way to keep connected.

A woman who lives thousands of miles away from your church is seeking to learn about Jesus. She is not a Christian and is looking for safe ways to privately learn about the Christian faith. She searches the internet with various search words of interest, just so happens to find a particular sermon on your church website, and reads it. She browses the rest of the website and reads about what your church believes. She also reads through the spiritual discussions on your online forums. She sees pictures of people having fun together, worshiping, and serving. She gets a sense of what it is to be a Christian and to be in a healthy church community. She may never post to your website or contact you in any way. She may only show up as a number on the website statistics page. Yet you are part of a process that ultimately leads her to Christ.

Web-Empowering Ministries

As the stories above indicate, a fully web-empowered church is able to minister 24/7 to anyone with internet access. The empowerment comes from combining the features of a variety of internet tools to more effectively deliver content that churches already have, enhance church administrative functions, and connect people in community.

Don't be troubled about getting all the many available features on your church website. Creating an excellent church internet ministry involves persistence over time. Do your best to add appropriate features to your website as you are able and ready. Not every feature will fit your ministry or those you serve. As you continue to add features and content, your church will become increasingly web-empowered in its own way. You don't need to feel pressured— in fact, there is value in adding features slowly so that your church and visitors can learn the new features and grow along with your website. With the help of the Web-Empowered Church software, you can rapidly install features that took years to develop and refine.

> *Don't be troubled about getting all the many available features on your church website.*

The following sections describe ways you can empower various ministries in the church. In previous chapters, I explained the different web tools we have at our disposal to enhance church ministry. The creativity and challenge for us comes from mixing, matching, and using them in real ministry situations. This chapter contains different internet ministry ideas. Most of these ideas have been tried in real ministry situations. This chapter will also introduce you to several WEC ministry extensions and other TYPO3 extensions that can be used in ministry. The list below is not in a specific order, but the more common ministries are listed earlier. Please feel free to use the ideas exactly as they are, use them to trigger new and better ideas, or ignore them and create your own approaches. We are all learning and exploring.

Empower Sermon

Sermons are the most valuable content many churches have to offer on the web. A great deal of effort goes into them, their content is usually original (or at least is not copyrighted by an outside source), and most churches produce them every week. You can produce sermons in multiple formats including text, audio, and video and can deliver them as webpages, PDF files, RSS, and

Podcast. In our experience, the text version is most popular. Adding sermon text to a website is fairly easy if your pastor writes out sermons in detail, but more difficult if you need to transcribe them from audio recordings. Text also offers the huge advantage of being searchable—both on your website and across the internet. If you provide a text sermon, make it a printable version, because people often print sermons to read or give to others. If you use PDF to make a printable version, create webpages containing the ser-

Sermons are the most valuable content many churches have to offer on the web.

mon text for online viewing and to make the text searchable. Since an oral sermon translated verbatim can be choppy and unorganized, consider editing sermons to ensure they work well as written information. You may need to insert section titles and break blocks of text into paragraphs to help make the sermon more readable.

Audio and video also offer a chance to expand the audience because individual visitors generally have a preference for one particular format. For example, some people would never pause to read all the text from a sermon, but they would listen to sermon audio on an MP3 player while they exercise. RSS feeds that link to your text sermons or Podcast for audio or video sermons expand the audience to include people who prefer a certain method of delivery. Adding formats provides the platform for a larger audience.

You can also augment the sermon with additional features, such as a group or individual Bible study that references many of the same Scriptures. You could also include a poll question or even a survey to get people thinking about the sermon topic. Some churches include the bulletin with the other sermon resources because it includes the sermon outline and other related information. You can also include online community to encourage open discussion about the sermon topic. If the pastor is willing to participate in the discussion, then the community could be even more fruitful.

WEC has a sermon extension that supports these features and also archives sermon data, such as notes and PowerPoint files, that will not be made available publicly but fit well with the other sermon information. The result is a useful place to store all the sermon resources for later retrieval by those who have authorized access.

The sermon extension supports many different resources that you name and define. It will list resources, search for them, and display them. WEC also has an extension that can play audio MP3 files and one that can play Flash video. The Flash video extension automatically measures the connection speed of the visitor and selects between two encoded videos to provide the best video quality for the connection.

Empower Prayer

Prayer is an important part of any Christian ministry. Many churches track prayer requests and also have a group of people who pray specifically for the requests. A common way to gather prayer requests on a website is to use an e-mail form. An e-mail form is a webpage containing form fields that visitors fill out. When visitors complete the form, they submit it, and the contents of the form are automatically e-mailed to one or more designated e-mail addresses. E-mail forms are not completely secure—a person with the knowledge and network access could theoretically intercept the information. Interception is unlikely, but if you require a high level of confidentiality, you may not want to use web forms, or you may want to encrypt the data in some way. At most churches, the web alone will not meet all needs for requesting prayer, so provide a phone number people can call to request prayer.

For less personal requests, you can use a community prayer system. WEC provides one that uses a connector community. The advantage of community prayer is that people can share needs quickly and publicly, and the community can come together to support them and pray for their requests. In our experience, many people like to participate in this way. We get more prayer posts than any other type of post to our website. The most posted-to page on the website is a slight variation of our main prayer request page—the e-candle page. Visitors post a thought or prayer and light a virtual candle created with an animated GIF. Every posted message includes a candle, and all the candles flicker together. There are over one thousand e-candle messages posted by people from

The advantage of community prayer is that needs are shared quickly and publicly, and the community can come together to support people and pray for their requests.

around the world. Many of the messages are quite serious, related to loved ones who have passed away or are seriously ill, wars and soldiers, salvation of loved ones, and marriage problems. This page's dark colors and flickering candles convey a sense of seriousness.

The WEC software extension generates an online prayer request page where visitors can publicly post prayer requests. The most recent requests are listed at the top of the page. You can configure the extension to allow all visitors or only visitors with accounts to post requests. Visitors have the option of posting anonymously or with their names. (The requests are all posted publicly, but anonymous requests do not include the name of the requestor.) Once a request is posted and if the requestor is willing to receive responses, anyone viewing the requests has the option of sending a private personal note. The note is entered via a web form and automatically sent to the original poster via e-mail, so requestors who posted anonymously can receive personal notes while remaining anonymous. We have seen significant ministry happen as people in the community comfort and support visitors who share prayer requests. Many times they have been willing to share about facing similar challenges. For example, women who are in the midst of a difficult divorce have received supportive responses from other women in the same situation. This is community, and this connection would not have happened if not for community prayer.

The WEC software extension also supports sending the contents of all new prayer requests via e-mail when they are posted. Visitors subscribe to receive prayer requests via e-mail, and prayer team members use this feature in order to provide immediate prayer support. The extension also supports other administrative features such as automatically filtering inappropriate language, automatically deleting the oldest prayer requests after a specified time, and optionally requiring that a moderator review the request before it is posted publicly on the website.

Empower Teaching

One of the challenges at most churches is finding enough teachers. A creative solution is to offer classes online. Traditional classes where the teacher does most of the talking or classes that can be partitioned into non-interactive components are good choices for online classes. There are several online teaching systems that allow you to create classes. In our experience, most teachers prefer not to create online classes. They simply want to teach. An approach that many teachers prefer is to record the teaching in audio or video during each class. The online class works best if the teacher uses charts, which are commonly in PowerPoint. The web team can combine the audio or video with the charts to create an online class.

Traditional classes where the teacher does most of the talking or classes that can be partitioned into non-interactive components are good choices for online classes.

When the WEC first started trying this approach, I expected it to be very popular and for churches to begin posting classes this way. Yet a significant challenge to online teaching is keeping the classes copyright-free, which is required if they are posted publicly on the internet. Classes often follow through a copyrighted book or teachers use copyrighted material to supplement their class. All class material needs to be original, or you need to make arrangements with the publisher to allow copyrighted content online.

WEC has a ministry extension that allows you to create a presentation, such as a class, that uses audio or video with charts that change automatically during the presentation. While watching the class, a visitor can move forward and backward in the presentation, and the charts and video will follow along. This is a nice tool for the visitor watching the presentation. To create the class, you must convert the audio to MP3 format, the video to FLV format, and the charts to JPG format. Using these files and the designated times for the charts to change, the extension delivers an online presentation of a class on your website. You can create multiple online classes simply by recording teachers who are teaching each class, generating the necessary files, and using this extension. In our experience, if minimal video editing is needed, an online class can be created in about three times the duration of the class. So a one-hour class takes approximately three hours to create after it is recorded, and most of that time is spent capturing, editing, and rendering the video. Once posted, the class is available to anyone anytime.

Online classes offer some interesting opportunities and options that are worth trying:

1. Classes are totally online and include an online forum that allows attendees and the instructor to discuss the current class content. Extra class materials are also posted to the web. By using this method a teacher can support several classes at one time. You can arrange to have classes on a flexible schedule that allows students to take them at any time or pace, or you can set classes on a specific schedule.

2. The main content of the class is provided online, and the class meets in person on a periodic basis for interactive discussion about the current topic.

3. The class is offered normally, but attendees have the option of attending either the online class or the live-and-in-person class. The online class is also an excellent way to catch up if an attendee misses a class.

In support of either online or live classes, the website can list available courses with course descriptions, provide online sign-up for courses, help people track which courses they have taken, and provide a way to order resources such as books. For any online class, you could hold discussion through a forum, e-mail list, or chat. In addition, you could add online quizzes to test visitors' understanding.

Another way to disciple people is through an online Bible study. These are fairly common among churches, and some youth groups use them. Churches usually set up an online Bible study with an e-mail list or a forum to allow the group to communicate. The leader of the study periodically posts Scripture references and questions. Participants read the Scriptures and respond to the questions online. The group discusses the topic and the answers. This is a quick and easy approach to implement online discipleship.

The most effective use of the web for teaching children is equipping parents or guardians to teach their children.

Teaching younger children via the web can be more difficult because they may not be able to read what is on a computer screen, or they may not know how to operate a computer very well. If you have skills in programming in Flash, you can create games that teach Bible stories and concepts. The most effective use of the web for teaching children is equipping parents or guardians to teach their children. You can use the web to supply all kinds of teaching resources to augment what the children learn at church. In addition, parents may find an online forum helpful for discussing various parenting challenges.

Empower Devotionals

A devotional is a short writing or Bible verse that helps visitors focus on God on a regular basis. Daily devotionals are difficult to include in your web ministry because they require content every day. If you can keep up with the content generation, daily devotionals can be a powerful tool for personal growth for both adults and youth within your church. In order to share the load, multiple staff can generate the content and possibly enlist an unpaid servant team. One way to get started and simplify devotional content generation is to provide only a daily Scripture reference. Selecting Scripture references from a current course of study or from the sermon simplifies the selection process while reinforcing the current teaching. To encourage daily participation, offer the daily devotional via e-mail. The individual devotionals are entered well ahead of time, and the devotional for the current day is automatically e-mailed to subscribers the night before—usually shortly after midnight to ensure that it is available to those who wake up early. You can also provide the devotional on paper for people who do not have internet access.

Daily devotionals can be a powerful tool for personal growth for both adults and youth within your church.

WEC has a software extension that adds more features to a devotional. It includes the ability to send the devotional e-mail, but also generates a devotional page to which visitors go daily. The page changes automatically each day, and a visitor can navigate to previous or future days' pages. You can organize the content into multiple categories and set the content duration for any amount of time. For example, if you are studying biblical topics, name one category "topic" and include a summary of the current topic. Set this content to remain for several days, or even weeks, while content in other categories changes daily.

The extension also supports a personal journal where a visitor who is logged on can enter his or her own notes or thoughts. Visitors use the personal journal editor to enter and then nicely format their notes by setting text attributes like bold, italics, and color. Journal information is kept private. Visitors see only their own journal entries, and the entries are stored encrypted in the database for additional protection.

You can use the WEC discussion extension along with the devotional to add community discussion and group learning. This enables the community to ask questions and share personal insights related to the current devotional. We find that this feature provides additional incentive to come to the devotional page because visitors want to monitor the latest posts to the online discussion.

Empower Service

Encouraging service and connecting people to unpaid servant (volunteer) positions in a church can be challenging. People who want to get involved are not always sure of what the needs and opportunities are. You can help by including on the website a list describing the opportunities to serve and an e-mail form visitors can use to request more information or sign up to begin serving. You can also use the website to help keep track of where people are serving.

You can help by including on the website a list describing the opportunities to serve.

WEC has a software extension that automates much of this process. Leaders in the church enter servant opportunities, and each entry includes fields for the name of the opportunity, the name of the ministry, a description of the opportunity, the location of where the service will occur, the dates and times of service, any required qualifications or training, and the point of contact. Leaders can also associate each opportunity with one or more skills from a list configured according to a ministry's needs. The list can include any number of skills, interests, spiritual gifts, and strengths. Once a leader enters an opportunity into the list database, it immediately becomes available on the website. Visitors can browse though the list of opportunities or search for opportunities based on their own personal skills. For example, if a visitor selects "computers," most of the opportunities in the internet ministry will show up on the resulting list. Visitors can narrow the search by selecting multiple skills and searching for opportunities that match all the skills. Once visitors identify interesting opportunities, they can print out a list, or they can commit to the opportunity via a web form. When a visitor submits the form, an e-mail containing all the form information is sent to the service opportunity contacts and, optionally, to an administrator.

At Ginghamsburg, we have used this capability for several years to match hundreds of people per year to servant opportunities. We accommodate people who are without internet access or are unsure about using this feature by periodically setting up computers at the church and staffing them with people who can help. The helpers either perform the computer-based tasks needed to search and sign up for a servant opportunity or look over people's shoulders to help them through the process. This way, no one is left out. Using the print capability, helpers can provide personalized paper copies of opportunities so that people can take the list home, read through the opportunity descriptions, and come back later to sign up. If someone commits to an opportunity, the helper will give him or her a paper copy including details of the opportunity they chose.

Empower Evangelism

As Christians, we are called to offer Christ to those who do not know him. The web provides many ways to creatively and effectively communicate this message through words, graphics, animation, sound, and video. Every church website should include the message of salvation, even if it is only in an "about us" section describing what the church believes. Some churches choose a "questions and answers" (Q & A) format to address specific questions visitors may have. If you would like to use the Q & A format to answer many questions about salvation and perhaps the Bible, then a "knowledge base" may be helpful.

A knowledge base is a type of database designed for storing knowledge about a topic. Each entry in the knowledge base has a title (the question) and information (the answer to the question). WEC has a knowledge base extension that enables visitors to search for entries containing

The web provides many ways to creatively and effectively communicate the message of Christ through words, graphics, animation, sound, and video.

specific keywords or to browse entries by category. Visitors can see a list of all the categories, a list of the most recent entries, and a list of most frequently viewed entries. The WEC website knowledge base extension provides how-tos about various aspects of TYPO3 and WEC. You can also use this extension to set up a "frequently asked questions" (FAQ) page. This extension is beneficial when you have more entries than fit comfortably on a single webpage but is not very useful if there are only a few entries.

Bringing people to your website for the purpose of evangelism is a challenge. One way to help people find your website is to include content that search engines will index. I hope that churches around the world will flood the internet with content on their websites so that when visitors use a search engine to search for keywords or phrases, the results list will almost always include churches. At Ginghamsburg, visitors from other religions have sent us e-mail saying they found a sermon on our website by typing in a phrase. In two cases, the sermons were about other religions, and the visitors had questions and comments about what the sermon said about their religions. We had an opportunity to share why and how we follow Jesus.

I hope that churches around the world will flood the internet with content on their websites so that when visitors use a search engine to search for keywords or phrases, the results list will almost always include churches.

Another less-common but effective way to attract non-Christians to your website is to advertise on non-Christian websites. For example, you could purchase specific Google AdWords that provide a link to your website based on specific words visitors enter. This may be a viable approach for websites focused on evangelism.

As mentioned in chapter 4, the internet—specifically public online services that promote social networking—is the "perfect" mission field for evangelism. I encourage you to deliberately and methodically send missionaries and mission teams out into the internet to be "salt and light" in the world. Be careful to prepare people for this mission field, and send only mature Christians who can manage the various pressures and temptations. If churches around the world jump into the dirty and unhealthy places on the internet, then the internet will become a much safer place, people in great need will be helped, people will be introduced to Christ, and lives will be transformed as only Jesus can do. Many churches are concerned about the cost of ministries that reach out to others, and for most churches internet evangelism is free because people who could become internet missionaries already have internet access. We need to equip and send them.

Empower Care

The web is usually not the right place to address serious care issues such as counseling and support groups. These are best done in person. A key reason for web-empowering a church is to allow the congregation to have more time for face-to-face ministry, such as counseling and support groups, by taking care of time-consuming details using the web. You can use the church website to provide basic support to care ministries by including care-related resources such as online teaching, contact information for support organizations, and dates and times for various care-related events. Use your website to list meeting information for local support groups. Also, for less severe cases, a private online forum or e-mail list can enable a support group to stay in contact and keep each other accountable between face-to-face meetings.

A key reason for web-empowering a church is to allow the congregation to have more time for face-to-face ministry.

Empower Missions

Since mission activities usually occur at a distance from a church, people in the church may not fully understand or relate to missions. The web can make the connection by helping people in the church understand missions and helping missionaries feel a closer relationship with the people who support them.

We were surprised by the number of missionaries who have computers and internet access. Even if missionaries do not have internet access, include a page on the church website for introducing visitors to the missionaries and missions that the church supports. Photos and maps are valuable communicators. Be sure to add missionaries to the page only with their permission; sometimes inclusion could expose them to dangerous or awkward situations. If missionaries have internet access and it is safe to include them, they can also post news or a periodic newsletter on the missions page.

Missionaries who would like more communication and interactivity might find a blog helpful. By using a blog, missionaries can keep the church up-to-date in a less formal and more personal way. Visitors can comment on the blog to communicate back to the missionary. The decision to use a blog depends on the interest and willingness of the missionary. For missionaries who prefer to write less frequently or are in locations that would make blogging on the public internet unwise, use a connector to create a missionary prayer page where only missionaries can post. We have done this, and the missionaries appreciated it. People from the church who want to support missions can subscribe to receive the missionaries' requests via e-mail. Missionaries say that they like being able to post a prayer request knowing that people in the church will be praying for it soon afterward because sometimes missionary prayer needs are urgent. Missionaries in more dangerous environments appreciate the protection provided by the anonymous post capability. They can still post prayer requests, but the general public does not need to know who or where they are.

If you'd like to try something interesting and fun, schedule a live chat with a missionary who has a reliable high-speed internet connection. You can even hold the chat during a meeting about missions. You can talk to the missionary via free voice-over-ip software such as Skype or Gizmo. Missionaries with web cameras can send live video for you to display on a large screen. I use these technologies to do live remote presentations and am amazed at how well this works. These applications are free and fairly easy to setup.

Internet tools can make mission trips come alive for the people back home. You can promote mission trips on the church website, and visitors can sign up for them there. If the mission team has

Internet tools can make mission trips come alive for the people back home.

access to the internet during the trip, they can create a mission trip blog to document each day of the trip. This allows people back home to follow the status of each day's activities and pray for current requests, such as someone becoming ill or transportation breaking down. It is good to keep the church informed and ask members to pray for those who are participating in the trip.

A mission trip photo gallery is also very popular, and TYPO3 includes several photo gallery extensions. If someone on the team has a digital camera and can upload photos during the trip, visitors monitoring the trip can view the photos. Sometimes the connection to the internet is good enough to support a blog but not good enough to post large photo files. In these cases, we post the photos when the team returns, and they are still a popular feature. Mission trip photos tend to be especially interesting and thought-provoking.

We usually leave the blog and photos on the website long after the trip. These tools can help people who are interested in future mission trips to understand what their trip may be like.

Empower Hospitality

One of the greatest barriers keeping new visitors from coming to a church is that they do not know what to expect. A website can give a new visitor the opportunity to learn about a church without the stress and time associated with an actual visit. One powerful feature to extend hospitality is a virtual tour that allows people to go through the steps of visiting the church and learn what will happen along the way. The tour should include practical steps that most visitors are concerned about, like where to park, where to enter the church, where to enter with a wheelchair, where to take kids of different ages, how kids will be signed in, how parents will be contacted if their kids need them, what to wear, where the restrooms are, what the seating options are, what first-time visitors are asked to do, where assistance can be found, what some of the people they are likely to meet will look like, what the worship style will be, and so on. I would love a feature like this if I were looking for a new church.

A website can give a new visitor the opportunity to learn about a church without the stress and time associated with an actual visit.

A virtual tour does not require fancy technology. You can implement it with a straightforward series of webpages. Instructions and pictures, including maps of the area and of the inside of the church, are critical. Knowing how to create video or Flash is beneficial, but the information is what is most important. Some churches include a 360-degree virtual experience of their sanctuary. Although this is fun, it is typically expensive to have done and shows only one room from one central point. I do not recommend doing this unless you want one simply because it is interesting.

Empower Ministry Teams

With people's busy schedules, it often becomes difficult for ministry teams to meet in person. Two internet tools are helpful for many different teams in the church. First, private forums or e-mail lists are handy for functions like keeping in touch, asking individuals to do certain tasks, reporting status, planning events, sharing prayer requests, and teaching. Second, for ministries that need to exchange files within the team, a private file-sharing tool is useful. Private file sharing allows common files to be both exchanged and archived. For example, teachers can share teaching materials.

For groups—the church staff, main church leaders, boards, and church members—an intranet may also be a valuable tool. An intranet is a private set of webpages accessible only to members of the group. It could include training, policy information, forms, lists of members, a forum, minutes from meetings, and a calendar. If you implement an intranet, make plans for keeping the list of members up-to-date to ensure that the correct people have access and unauthorized people do not.

For groups—the church staff, main church leaders, boards, and church members —an intranet may also be a valuable tool.

Empower Newsletters

Many churches use monthly or quarterly newsletters to communicate with attendees. Newsletters are important communication tools, but paper versions are costly to produce and mail. An electronic version has several advantages over paper. You can make an online newsletter longer and more colorful because, unlike using paper and ink, webpages with color do not cost extra. As I like to remind my friends who are print designers, our pictures can move and talk—online newsletters can include audio, video, and Flash. You can send them out more frequently and therefore include more timely information. If you keep it fairly short, you can send an online newsletter every week at a specific day and time and be very effective. One newsletter per week is probably enough for most people to receive in their e-mail inbox.

There are three types of delivery mechanisms for online newsletters:

1. Post the newsletter contents on the church website. This allows you to create a full-featured newsletter that includes various web features.
2. Send the contents via e-mail. One challenge with e-mail is that different e-mail programs display HTML e-mail differently, so limit e-mail newsletters to simple HTML features. One advantage of e-mail is that it comes to the visitor's mailbox without the visitor having to take any additional action.
3. Combine the first two options: post the majority of the newsletter on the website, but send a starter e-mail to all subscribers. This option has the advantages of the other two options. The starter e-mail should be a simple HTML e-mail that will display correctly using most e-mail software. It should contain the theme of the newsletter, titles of the online contents, and many links back to the church website. Some of the links should go to new information, but others should go to commonly used features of the website. The newsletter notifies website visitors of new content and promotes the website by reminding visitors of various features and getting them accustomed to going to the web for church information.

TYPO3 includes an extension that supports the process of creating an online newsletter and then sending that newsletter to a list of subscribers. One advantage of the extension is that you create the starter e-mail as just another page on the website. The webpage does not have links to it for general viewing, but creating the newsletter as a standard page makes the development process easier. Once the page is created, the extension processes the page to create the HTML e-mail, which it then sends out to the subscribers at the scheduled date and time.

With any e-mail sent from the web server, there is the possibility that subscriber spam filters may block the e-mail. Spam filters are programs that run on a mail server or on a visitor's local computer and attempt to determine whether or not each e-mail is unwanted advertising or some other unsolicited e-mail. Spam filters have many set-up options, but if a filter suspects an e-mail is spam, it will usually move the e-mail to a special folder. The subscriber may never see that e-mail. As you create the template for your starter e-mail, test spam filters by sending the e-mail to different e-mail accounts. The rules for getting e-mail through spam filters change as spammers develop new techniques and spam filters counter them. If filters become a problem, you may want to test more often, or you may want to switch to a very simple e-mail. In addition, encourage subscribers to whitelist your e-mail address. Whitelisting tells the spam filter software to allow e-mails from the specified e-mail address to pass through the spam filter without being checked. Some visitors do not have access to their spam whitelist, and many visitors may not know how to make this change; however, those who are successful will receive your e-mails. To further complicate the issue, many countries have antispam laws that vary and change and that may impact the bulk e-mail you send.

In every bulk e-mail, I suggest that you include instructions and a link to help people unsubscribe from the e-mail list. Also include the name, mailing address, and phone number for your church at the bottom of each e-mail. This is desirable internet etiquette. Your e-mail is clearly not spam, but these two items are commonly requested within antispam laws and help identify that your e-mail is not spam. As you begin to send many e-mails at a time, you will need to ensure that the e-mail is fully compliant with the latest spam laws and guidelines. Copies of the spam laws from around the world can be found at SpamLaws.com. Some larger internet providers may have additional rules to follow for multiple e-mails sent to their subscribers, and they can block all e-mails from your domain if they suspect you are sending spam.

In every bulk e-mail, include instructions and a link to help people unsubscribe from the e-mail list. Also include the name, mailing address, and phone number for your church.

Empower Leader Communications

Newsletters are a common way for leaders to communicate with those they serve; however, for more direct communications, a leader may want to use a blog. As mentioned before, this is an excellent way for youth leaders to communicate with students. In fact, it is a way many of them choose to communicate already. In addition, churches sometimes include pastors' blogs on their websites. A pastor's blog is included by default in the initial installation of the WEC-TYPO3 software. If a pastor's blog is created, it is important that the pastor knows how to blog and is committed to keeping the blog updated. A blog can become a burden to a pastor unless the pastor naturally likes to write and communicate by writing. Another leadership empowerment tool is a group chat with a ministry leader. If you use group chat, it may be easier to have a fast typist support the leader so the leader has more time to think without needing to type. A group chat is especially useful when there is a special church-wide issue to discuss, such as a church building project. If the chat conversation would be of interest to others, be sure to post a transcript of the conversation on your website.

For more direct communications, a leader may want to use a blog.

Empower Events

It seems that churches are all about people participating in events. You can announce and describe events on the website, and you can also place them on an online calendar. As the calendar grows, it is beneficial to use a calendar that can be limited to display only events in specific categories defined by each visitor. For example, if a visitor has no children, they may prefer not to see youth events on the calendar. Another popular calendar feature is the ability to copy events from the online church calendar to a local calendar on the visitor's computer. For example, the events on the church calendar can be automatically inserted into a visitor's Microsoft Outlook calendar and loaded onto a handheld device like a Personal Digital Assistant (PDA).

Online event registration is also valuable. This feature includes web forms that collect the needed information and send it to the appropriate person via e-mail, store it in a database, or both. More powerful event registration applications can perform functions like limiting registrations to a specified total number, providing rosters of registrants for events, and archiving information on who attended which event.

The most technically challenging feature to support event registra-

The most technically challenging feature to support event registration is online sales.

tion is online sales. Sales include purchasing products, like a book needed for a course of study, or paying a fee for participating in a conference. Online-store software is fairly common, and TYPO3 offers some solutions; however, online stores are typically more difficult to set up than other web features.

The two biggest challenges when setting up an online store are purchasing a Secure Socket Layer (SSL) certificate and installing it, and getting a merchant account and setting up the software to use it. You must purchase the SSL certificate through a lengthy process that includes verifying your church's identity. The certificate is also fairly expensive. The certificate is actually just a long list of numbers used to identify your website and to enable it to securely exchange private information (like credit card numbers) over the internet. The merchant account enables processing of credit cards and other electronic forms of exchanging money. A merchant account connects to your church's bank account to transfer funds to and from that account. A merchant account costs money, and each online transaction costs money.

There are companies that offer solutions to simplify the store setup process. Some offer preconfigured online stores, and some offer only transaction processing. These solutions usually take visitors to another website to make the purchase. Your hosting company may also offer support for online stores. Any of these may be viable solutions for your church; however, providing a full online store locally on your website offers the best and most intuitive experience for a visitor making a purchase.

Empower Fellowship

Online fellowship and community happen when people connect online. As churches become more web-empowered, many of the website features will enhance fellowship and community. A set of forums where people can gather and communicate is valuable. You can create a few forums that represent common interests for your church. We have a forum called "fellowship," where people from the church can talk about any healthy subject they choose. This forum works well, and the title of the forum encourages healthy connections.

As churches become more web-empowered, many of the website features will enhance fellowship and community.

E-cards are another way to connect people to people. E-cards are personal electronic greeting cards. Like traditional greeting cards, you can use them for birthdays, weddings, anniversaries, sympathy, encouragement, and more. You can also use them to invite people to church or special events such as Christmas, Easter, or a festival. We create our e-cards using Flash. A visitor who wants to send an e-card selects a card, fills in the destination name and e-mail address, enters a personal message for the inside of the card, previews the card online, and then sends the card. The person receiving the card receives a notification via e-mail that contains a unique link that takes him or her back to the website to view the card. Hosting the e-card on the website helps ensure that the e-card displays and works correctly. With Flash, the cards can include sound, animation, video, and links.

Empower Small Groups

Small groups, sometimes called "cell groups," meet periodically for activities such as fellowship, Bible study, serving, support, and fun. A website can empower small-group ministry by connecting visitors with existing groups in the church. An easy way to do this is to provide an e-mail form that collects information to help match visitors to small groups. A person who knows the available small groups well reviews the e-mail contents, identifies appropriate small groups, and contacts the visitor with specific suggestions. Another option is to include information on the website such as when and where groups meet, the main focus of each group, the ages and family situation of group members, and the contact information for the leaders. A visitor

A website can empower small-group ministry by connecting visitors with existing groups in the church.

can contact a group leader via e-mail or a web form. To protect the leaders' privacy, do not provide their addresses, phone numbers, or personal e-mails on the website; instead, implement e-mail aliases that forward to personal e-mail addresses. For example, an e-mail address like SouthFamilyGroup@yourchurch.org could forward to the personal e-mail address of the leader of the South family small group. A web application can also enable small-group leaders to provide membership and attendance information back to the church.

There are many opportunities for enhancing small groups once they are established. Examples include a private forum, a calendar, a photo gallery, a list of news and announcements, a prayer list, and more. As long as you keep the information private and accessible only within the group, and as long as you have permission, group members can share personal information. The private small group area could include addresses, phone numbers, birthdays, and anniversaries. This brings the group closer and keeps them connected between meetings.

Empower Stewardship

If you have an online store, you can take donations online. The dilemma of accepting online giving is that most online purchases are done using credit cards and most people do not pay off their credit cards each month, so online giving may

Online giving may promote debt, which is not typically something churches want to promote.

promote debt, which is not typically something churches want to promote. One possible solution is to support only those methods of online payment that do not involve credit such as e-checks or debit cards, but these may be more difficult to set up and to enforce.

With proper security measures (such as SSL) in place, there are opportunities for managing the church finances online and for tracking gifts to the church. A useful feature to compliment online giving is to allow visitors access to a summary of all their tithes, offerings, and items donated to the church. This, too, can be challenging to implement.

Empower Memorials

For hundreds of years, churches have provided memorials for people who have gone to be with the Lord. Traditionally, memorials have been in the form of long-lasting items such as stones, plaques, or trees. Online memorials are a unique way to continue the tradition. I credit Leonard Sweet, author of this book's foreword, with this concept. We have tried it at Ginghamsburg, and it has worked well. In general, people think online memorials are a good idea, but for some, it is a bit too different to consider, especially in a time of grieving. Given the features that the web can provide and the fact that people can access the memorial from anywhere on the internet, I expect these to become more popular.

Online memorials can include many different features. The memorials at Ginghamsburg include a main photo and a short life story, with options for a picture gallery, a video, and a reflections page. The reflections page allows visitors to post comments and thoughts whenever they would like to post them. We have agreed to host the online memorials for as long as the technology allows.

CHAPTER 11

WHERE ARE WE GOING NEXT?

Visions of internet ministry and the Web-Empowered Church

The world is becoming increasingly connected, initially through computers and wired connections, but now through wireless connections and other devices. Everything is connecting to the internet—houses, cars, televisions, video recorders, cameras, watches, appliances, and more. The increasingly ubiquitous internet connectivity and worldwide connectedness provide many new ministry opportunities for a web-empowered church. We just need to be there.

In time, all ministries in a church will include a web component of some kind, and we won't think much about it. Internet technology will support the day-to-day operation of our churches and will provide the bidirectional communication mechanisms necessary to deliver ministries to the people churches serve as well as to evangelize non-Christians around the world. The internet will allow the church to connect and become more integrated into people's lives according to their specific needs. For example, instead of printing the current week's Bible study on paper, the church will automatically deliver it to each subscriber's handheld device. The message, the mission, and the people remain the same, so the internet will not force churches to create all-new content. The ways in which the content is packaged, delivered, and received will change, and churches will be able to reach more people and meet the specific needs of the people they serve. This is about using technology to minister better. These ideas are not innovative or unique. These are technology trends that are happening and will happen in other areas of life; it is up to churches and ministries to be there, too— and maybe even lead a bit!

WEC Making the Future Happen

The Web-Empowered Church (WEC) is part of a movement among God's people in churches around the world partnering together to help apply internet technology that will take the church into the future. The WEC is developing powerful web-based, ministry-

The mission of WEC is to innovatively apply web technology to empower the worldwide church for ministry.

enhancing tools to empower ministries now and prepare the church for increasing impact in the future. WEC is a ministry of the Foundation for Evangelism, located in Lake Junaluska, North Carolina, USA. The mission of WEC is to innovatively apply web technology to empower the worldwide church for ministry. WEC plans to web-empower over ten thousand churches by 2010.

If this sounds exciting to you, please consider joining other Christians around the world to help expand WEC's reach and get WEC capabilities into churches and ministries. Please use the free ministry tools and resources provided by WEC and TYPO3. The tools will not fulfill their ministry purposes until they are deployed on church and ministry websites.

More about WEC

The following list of characteristics helps define the attitude and intent of the WEC ministry. It also helps distinguish WEC from other solutions for your web ministry. As I think you will see, WEC is quite different from most other solutions in several ways.

Movement among God's People: We believe that WEC is part of a movement of God's people around the world; and the full success of WEC will not be realized unless God's people join in the development, deployment, and use of WEC and TYPO3. Since this is a movement, we look to the Holy Spirit for guidance to achieve this God-sized mission.

Love for the Church: We believe that the church and church attendees are God's hands and feet and God's primary provision for introducing people to Christ, discipling them, and caring for them. As a result, this movement is designed to equip local churches and connect people to local churches. Also, we don't advocate web-only churches, but we do believe that the internet can make churches of all types more effective.

Global Thinking: The target users for WEC are Christians anywhere in the world. This is part of the reason we chose TYPO3, which was developed mainly in Europe. Both TYPO3 and the WEC extensions support multiple languages. WEC is a system for all God's people.

Love of Diversity and Creativity: We praise God for diversity in churches and diversity in people. We praise God for the creativity applied in our creation and the creative ways that God's people implement church. The WEC celebrates diversity and attempts to support and make provisions for different types, styles, methods, races, cultures, denominations, and languages of churches around the world.

Conduit, Not Content: We celebrate the creativity and uniqueness of pastors, church staff, and lay servants who create the content for their churches and internet ministry. We consider the WEC to be the conduit that can present, share, and amplify that rich content. For this reason, the WEC generates very little website content. The content will come from God's people, who will share it more easily and more fully via WEC tools.

Taking the Church to New Levels: The WEC tools help take churches far beyond current static church websites to interactive web applications that amplify the impact of most of the ministries in the church. Through WEC research, WEC is developing new and innovative ways to apply web technology in ministry. WEC extensions are taking the church to the next step in internet ministry and are posturing the church for the future.

Community Support: The WEC development team is providing extensive resources to help churches with web ministry. However, one-on-one help will come from the WEC community through the forums, user groups, and individuals and organizations that join in the movement. After you use WEC for a while, please consider jumping in and helping others. This approach will allow WEC to grow around the world to thousands of churches and ministries.

Ministry Focused: WEC is not about technology. It is about practical tools for ministry. We strive to design tools that regular people in regular churches can use. The WEC tools are developed in partnership with churches that have demonstrated ministry excellence and use the tools in real world situations.

No Requirement to Promote WEC: WEC does not require a link back to the WEC website to promote the ministry, although we appreciate links because they support the movement. We are servants of Jesus Christ. If the WEC system is used for the Kingdom, then that is what matters. Please use it for ministry and promote WEC only as you choose.

Free Software: WEC software, online documentation, and training are free to all Christian churches and ministries. Of course, donations to the Foundation for Evangelism, the sponsor of WEC, or hosting with Vine Hosting are helpful, but that is your choice. Please note that churches will likely need to pay for features like website hosting, domain names, rights to use content or graphics from other sources, special training or consulting, books, and certificates for e-commerce. Other organizations supply these features.

Hosting Choice: WEC does not require that churches host with a specific hosting company. Any server that can meet the hardware and software requirements can run WEC software. Also, churches can move their websites to different hosting companies as long as they move to a server that can run WEC software. WEC software can run on several types of common web servers. WEC will not force you into a specific hosting situation.

No "Cookie Cutter" Websites: WEC tools are designed to be adapted to meet different churches' needs and preferences. WEC celebrates the uniqueness of individual churches and enables heavy customization of both style and features. Your church website does not need to look like every other WEC-based website. Of course, churches using the same WEC templates will look similar, but churches also have the option of creating totally new templates of their own.

Community Websites: WEC strives to provide features that allow people to interact with the website and with each other in community. Ministry often happens in community, and churches are healthier when the people are in community together. WEC desires to help connect the body of believers in a church.

Powerful: WEC strives to create the most powerful web-based ministry tools in the world. Traditionally, capabilities like those provided by WEC and TYPO3 were available only to larger churches that could afford them or develop them. But we want even very small churches to have the full power and opportunity of a system like this, and the ability to grow their web ministries incrementally over time. The power makes a small website easier to manage and prepares the church for the future.

Innovation: WEC is always looking for creative ways to enhance ministry impact within churches. We strive to unleash the God-given creativity in God's people and to use it for God's glory. We are constantly pushing ourselves to try new ideas, even if they could fail as we test them. WEC is changing the way web ministry is done and is empowering churches for more effective ministry.

Technology Savvy: WEC strives to remain on the cutting edge of technology and current web trends. We believe that an excellent church website maximizes use of available technology. At the same time, ministry comes first, so we will not use technology that adversely impacts visitors. We want to be technologically savvy to apply the latest technology when it is of value, but also not to apply it when it is not of value.

Excellence and Openness: WEC has developers who are passionate Christians and are very technically skilled. They are prepared for the challenge and committed to excellence. However, we have made and will continue to make mistakes along the way. Some of the mistakes may be large. We will share this information openly and will fix mistakes as best and as quickly as we can because we want churches to have excellent tools.

Recognition of the Challenge: We acknowledge that meeting the goals of WEC is an incredible challenge. There is a lot of sophisticated software to develop and maintain. There is research to do. There is documentation and training to develop. And we are supporting thousands of churches around the world. Clearly, the task ahead is huge. But WEC is a God thing. We have already seen God's provision take us farther and faster than expected. Churches around the world are already using WEC and are ministering more effectively as a result. So we look for and expect God's continued guidance and provision for the future. And we continue to do the difficult tasks because this is for Jesus Christ.

Blessed to Serve: We are blessed to be servants of Jesus Christ and want nothing other than to be in God's will and plan. We work hard to support God's kingdom around the world by helping Christians in churches and ministries apply internet technology to ministry. WEC is a serving ministry. We are blessed to serve.

WEC Technology

Web-empowering the church requires the development of a large set of powerful web applications that can be readily obtained, configured, and deployed on individual church websites. The technical foundation for making this possible is a full-featured Content Management System (CMS). Within WEC, the CMS is similar to an operating system (like Microsoft Windows or Linux) for web applications. The CMS manages usernames, controls access, stores the content, manages files, integrates web applications ("extensions"), and provides a common look and feel. The CMS that WEC uses and requires is called "TYPO3." Kasper Skårhøj, a committed Christian in Copenhagen, Denmark, leads TYPO3 development.

Within WEC, the CMS is similar to an operating system for web applications.

There is great advantage in commonality. The commonality that Microsoft Windows users experience can be a value that TYPO3 users experience. Since many people use Microsoft Windows on their computers, those people can easily exchange files and programs, and developers can create programs that will run on many different computers as long as the computers run Microsoft Windows. Using TYPO3 across many church websites has similar advantages. TYPO3 allows churches to share web applications and developers to write web applications that many churches can use. It also enables common documentation, training, conferences, and user groups.

While no software is perfect, including TYPO3, it was critical that we make a choice for a CMS. WEC chose TYPO3 for several reasons, and, in fact, it was the only CMS that met all the criteria.

God's Provision: Throughout the WEC effort, we look for God's provision and the leading of the Holy Spirit. Kasper Skårhøj, TYPO3's developer, has said, "Whatever my creativity can produce is meant to honor God since he gave me my talent in the first place. For me that translates into the vision of giving my best through TYPO3 to the world." Through careful study and prayer, we believe TYPO3 is God's provision for à foundation to web-empower the church.

Content Entry by Less Technical People: A common bottleneck preventing updates to church websites is the availability of the person who can do the updating. With TYPO3, not only one person, but a team of content maintainers can update the website. TYPO3 offers a configurable access control capability that allows an administrator to specify exactly what pages and content each content maintainer is allowed to update. A simple editor allows the content maintainer to update his or her content from anywhere on the internet using a standard web browser. Churches can hold updates pending approval and can undo mistakes. These features are critical to maintaining fresh and accurate content on the church website.

Multilingual: WEC equips churches around the world, which requires the built-in TYPO3 multilingual capability. This capability also includes support for multiple character sets because many languages have unique characters. The core TYPO3 software and extensions already support many different languages, so even the backend administrator's pages are available in different languages.

Dynamic Content: Keeping a church website up-to-date is difficult. The ability to set the start and end dates for content, causing it to automatically appear and disappear from the website, can alleviate some of the content maintenance burden. Also, many churches have content that should be accessible only to specified groups such as board members, lay leaders, or staff. TYPO3 offers these capabilities.

Extension Installation: Extensions are web applications that can be placed on a website. WEC provides new and upgraded ministry extensions that a church can easily incorporate into an existing church website without a series of complicated installation steps or someone with special skills. TYPO3's method of incorporating separate extensions simplifies installation. Extensions are stored in an online extension repository by the extension developers. Anyone using TYPO3 can use the extension manager module within TYPO3 to download new or updated extensions from the online repository. The process automatically copies the files and makes the appropriate database updates. Previously installed extensions can be uninstalled with a few mouse clicks. This feature allows WEC to create and distribute extensions cleanly and easily to churches around the world.

Templates: Churches need templates to establish and change the look and feel of their websites with minimal effort. We don't want to force churches to have websites that all look similar. TYPO3 offers a template capability called TemplaVoila that is versatile in the creation of the layout, the style, and the dynamically-created navigation. Though creating custom templates requires additional technical skills, just about any possible layout can be created in TYPO3's templating system.

Hosting Options: Churches should not be tied to a specific hosting option. With TYPO3, churches can use turnkey hosting companies that preinstall WEC and TYPO3, host on a dedicated server at a hosting company, or host on a computer at their church. TYPO3 runs on most common web servers including LAMP and WAMP servers. When there is a need to move to a new server computer, TYPO3 can export the database and then import it into another computer running TYPO3. The import/export capability can also support sharing of TYPO3 extensions, settings, and content.

Free: Churches must keep costs to a minimum. TYPO3 is free via an open source General Purpose License (GPL). In addition, it can run on web servers that run all free open source software. With TYPO3 running on a LAMP-based computer, a fully capable web server can execute all of WEC without any cost to acquire any software. All the software is open source—available for free, including source code.

Highly Capable: TYPO3 is extremely powerful and is already used on thousands of websites around the world. Due to its origins in Denmark, it is most popular among commercial websites in Europe. TYPO3 is proven technology. It already supports websites with thousands of pages, thousands of users, and many interactive features. Starting with the power of TYPO3 enables WEC to leap forward to provide powerful capabilities to churches, and for WEC development to focus on ministry extensions instead of enhancing the common CMS.

Support: As with any sophisticated system, TYPO3 can be challenging for the people who are setting it up and configuring it, so both the TYPO3 development community and WEC are providing additional support and tools to help simplify administration of TYPO3. Content entry is easy to learn; the challenge comes with configuring the many settings and options that reflect TYPO3's many capabilities. TYPO3 includes far more documentation than most open source projects. The Web-Empowered Church provides additional documentation and training as well as online support communities. Churches using TYPO3-WEC are part of a worldwide Christian support community.

Conclusion

Web-empowering your church is not easy, just as most significant ministry is not easy, but you are not alone. The growing community of Web-Empowered Church servants from around the world is accessible now at WebEmpoweredChurch.com. For developers who help create and enhance the Web-Empowered Church software, documentation, and training, the website is available at WebEmpoweredChurch.org. There two websites—WebEmpowered Church.com for end-users and WebEmpoweredChurch.org for developers—so end-users do not have to sort through the technical programming discussion. (Even if you are not a developer, we encourage you to go to the developer website to help us define requirements for WEC extensions.) This community is a team for Jesus and part of a movement of God. WEC is not pushing you toward a specific Christian theology or type of church. WEC wants to empower you to do your Christian ministry in your unique way.

Most significant ministry is not easy.

Please pray this prayer with me:

Heavenly Father, Creator and Redeemer, we pray for those of us in the Web-Empowered Church movement as we seek to empower our churches for ministry using internet technology. This is a new and difficult challenge that needs your guidance and wisdom to succeed. Help our churches welcome this new ministry, and help our church leaders and website visitors embrace technology as a tool for ministry. Help us use the web to expand evangelism, discipleship, and care throughout the world. And when the magnitude of the challenge feels bigger than we are, please help us to rely on you and to step forward boldly to do your will to the best of our abilities. Please protect and bless the efforts of the Web-Empowered Church community of researchers, developers, testers, trainers, and users around the world. We are your servants and are blessed to serve you in internet ministry.

—In Jesus' name, Amen.

USING THE CD-ROM

This CD-ROM includes content from www.WebEmpowered Church.com that is useful for learning TYPO3 and WEC Extensions. We provide the CD-ROM because some of the files are quite large and can be difficult to download, especially if you have a modem connection to the internet. You can check online for updates to the CD-ROM content at www.WebEmpowered Church.com/CDROM.

CD-ROM Contents

Presentation: A presentation about the Web-Empowered Church presented by Mark Stephenson, the Director of the Web-Empowered Church ministry. This page also demonstrates the WEC presentation extension that you can use on your website.

Getting Started Doc: The WEC Getting Started document will introduce you to Web-Empowered Church, to using TYPO3, and to other opportunities for learning and support.

Tutorials: Learn about TYPO3 and extensions that you can use on your website. Each tutorial is made up of a sequence of WEC How-tos that cover a specific topic.

How-tos: The How-tos help you find detailed answers to common questions. In addition, How-tos include Flash movies that show you the steps as you would see them on your screen. Note: viewing these presentations requires the Adobe (Macromedia) Flash Player installed on your computer.

WEB-TYPO3 Install: Instructions to install, run, and uninstall the WEB Starter Package, TYPO3, and a full web server on your computer.

Link to Online Book Pages: The book pages on the Web-Empowered Church website. Here, listed by book chapter and section, you will find: website links, additional details and information, and updates to the book contents. You can also access the online discussion forum.

Software Requirements

Viewing and using the files on this CD-ROM requires:

- A PC running Windows (see below for other computers)
- A standard up-to-date web browser such as Internet Explorer or Mozilla Firefox
- Adobe Flash Player (Version 9 or later)
- Adobe Reader (Version 6 or later)
- Unzip utility or Windows XP

Starting the CD-ROM

Put the CD-ROM in a Windows-based computer. The computer should read the CD-ROM and automatically start the computer's default web browser. The web browser will display the CD-ROM start page. All the pages and files on the CD-ROM are viewed within a web browser and can be accessed via links on the webpages.

If the web browser does not start automatically, you can go to the main directory of the CD-ROM and click on the Start.exe file to execute it. The CD-ROM includes a simple web server from Server2Go (www.Server2Go-web.de) that displays the webpages. When you exit your web browser, the server will automatically stop executing.

Macs and Other Computers: For Macs and other computers not running Windows, the pages can be viewed using a web browser and opening the index.html file in the htdocs directory of the CD-ROM. This will allow you to view the entire contents of the CD-ROM. You cannot install and run the WEC-TYPO3 Server because the software requires a Windows-based PC. Instead, you can go to the Web-Empowered Church Install Page (www.WebEmpowered Church.com/gettingstarted/installing) for instructions on how to install the WEC Starter Package on your computer or a web server.